Growth Mindset

A Can-do Approach to Building Confidence

(A Guide to Personal Growth and Self Esteem Mastery Develop Your Success Qualities)

George Hendry

Published By **Darby Connor**

George Hendry

All Rights Reserved

Growth Mindset: A Can-do Approach to Building Confidence (A Guide to Personal Growth and Self Esteem Mastery Develop Your Success Qualities)

ISBN 978-1-7752436-4-9

No part of this guidebook shall be reproduced in any form without permission in writing from the publisher except in the case of brief quotations embodied in critical articles or reviews.

Legal & Disclaimer

The information contained in this book is not designed to replace or take the place of any form of medicine or professional medical advice. The information in this book has been provided for educational & entertainment purposes only.

The information contained in this book has been compiled from sources deemed reliable, and it is accurate to the best of the Author's knowledge; however, the Author cannot guarantee its accuracy and validity and cannot be held liable for any errors or omissions. Changes are periodically made to this book. You must consult your doctor or get professional medical advice before using any of the suggested remedies, techniques, or information in this book.

Upon using the information contained in this book, you agree to hold harmless the Author from and against any damages, costs, and expenses, including any legal fees potentially resulting from the application of any of the information provided by this guide. This disclaimer applies to any damages or injury caused by the use and application, whether directly or indirectly, of any advice or information presented, whether for breach of contract, tort, negligence, personal injury, criminal intent, or under any other cause of action.

You agree to accept all risks of using the information presented inside this book. You need to consult a professional medical practitioner in order to ensure you are both able and healthy enough to participate in this program.

Table Of Contents

Chapter 1: What Is Mindset? 1

Chapter 2: Why Is Mindset Important? .. 11

Chapter 3: Fixed Vs Growth Mindset 21

Chapter 4: The Dangers Of A Fixed Mindset 32

Chapter 5: The Power Of A Growth Mindset 42

Chapter 6: Can You Change Your Mindset? 53

Chapter 7: Strategies To Develop A Growth Mindset 65

Chapter 8: How To Deal With Setbacks .. 75

Chapter 9: The Science Of Growth Mindset 86

Chapter 10: Truth Behind Growth Mindset 95

Chapter 11: Benefits Of Growth Mindset 105

Chapter 12: Transforming Your Mindset 114

Chapter 13: Developing Your Growth Mindset 127

Chapter 14: Difference Between Personality And Character 139

Chapter 15: 12 Pillars Of Character 144

Chapter 16: Be A Good Citizen - Good Citizen Vs Bad Citizen 164

Chapter 17: Be Yourself 171

Chapter 18: Can Character Be Taught? 178

Chapter 1: What Is Mindset?

The mind is an extremely efficient tool that will ultimately define who you are as an individual. It is also known as the mindset. the way you think or think about things, your mindset affects the way you think about the world around you and your own perception.

That's it. In essence it's the set of ideas and beliefs that affect your approach to every circumstance. The way you think about it can define your character, helping you figure out the situation in the world around you and how you need to do about it.

How Mindsets Are Formed

Since the dawn of time, individuals have thought, behaved and acted differently than the other. Most of the time the common sense suggests that such differences stem from the differences in one's environment or learning experience and even training. Research also suggests to the same conclusion.

While experiences, background and even training all are external, some internal variables such as genetics have an impact in.

The majority of experts agree today that the process of forming a mental mind is the result of combining both. In other words, even though each person has a distinct collection of genes the results of their education, experiences and efforts on their own will lead into consideration the entire route.

Your life experiences as well as genes together shape your beliefs and attitudes. In addition, since both play significant roles to play in your mental outlook and beliefs, it is helpful to learn how these two aspects are related to.

Your attitude towards something is what you feel or think about it. Especially as it reflects by the way you conduct yourself.

Your attitude could have a variety of elements, such as the emotional aspect or how people or things make you feel. There is also the cognitive aspect, which describes what you believe or feel about the topic. Then comes the behavioral part that shows what you do when faced by your person.

There are also your convictions, which are just the feeling of being certain about some thing. The basis of beliefs is ideas that, at a certain time, the ideas start becoming more certain, they become belief systems. They then influence your beliefs, and in turn influence your thinking.

Beliefs and attitudes then result in habits that reflect the way you think.

One of the most well-known and well-known example of this is to see that the glass is "half empty" or "half full".

Types of Mindsets

There are many types of mental models that could allow you to unleash your full potential or limit your possibilities. It's possible to have a lengthy list of them, but these are some that have been proven by studies. Let's take a look at these:

Abundance Mindset vs Scarcity Mindset

How you perceive your abundance and scarcity perceptions in the various aspects of your life will greatly affect your ability to succeed in life. Imagine that you and two other people walk along the sidewalk. They're chatting with one another, laughing, jokes and taking a breath in and out.

Are you thinking that either could be concerned that there might lack of oxygen available for each of them? Most likely not, as the air supply is abundant.

Put the same two individuals scuba diving together, and one of their tanks starts malfunctioning. This person is signaling the need for oxygen, and then the air around them is a valuable commodity.

It is possible that this shortage will cause the two to worry an anxiety that the oxygen supply isn't sufficient for both of the two of them?

The majority of most people appear to have more of an attitude of scarcity. Many people view their lives as a limited amount and, if they were forced to give away, it wouldn't suffice for them.

It is extremely difficult for these people to give accountability, respect, or even authority. They end up fighting for resources in the event that there is many of the latter.

But the people who have a positive outlook are not restricted by this mindset. Instead of seeing opportunities as a limited resource, they work to make more chances to themselves, and accept the change rather than avoiding it.

In the end the situation, someone who has a mindset of scarcity is one who has negative thoughts. They adopt an attitude of victimization. In reality, their daily concentration is focused on aspects that could not work.

However, those who have an abundance mentality tend to channel all of their resources into whatever they can do and think of many possibilities for improving their present situation.

Productive Mindset vs Defensive Mindset

This combination basically addresses the performance of every day. A lot of people believe that they are in a positive mindset or they're productive, but they're really just busy. In reality, they might not be productively completing tasks or completing their assignments.

Consider your day-to-day agenda and list the roughly ten things that you must complete at the end of the day. Perhaps you've spent the day rushing around doing things, but once it's five o'clock and you finish your day, you discover that you've only been able to complete three of the 10 things that you're supposed to accomplish.

It's like you're on the job every day, but you aren't getting much accomplished.

Is this a sign that you're not motivated and do not wish to reach your objectives? Perhaps it's due related to your attitude.

Being productive implies that you make use of everything you can, which includes your time, energy, and efforts in a productive method. However, it is also a sign that you aren't trying to do everything, cover all the ground or just do it the most efficient way.

It is about making the most of what's available, while having fun in it. The people who have a strong mentality seek out reliable information which can be verified and utilize their logic to make smart decisions.

In this way, they discover ways to improve their performance to spend more time figuring out methods to increase their efficiency rather than focusing on problems and becoming stuck.

However, the defensive mentality, as it's name implies, is self-protective as well as self-defensive. This kind of mentality only looks for information that it is accustomed to and is shut down if it perceives as being threatening. It is evident that this type of thought pattern could be very restrictive.

It's also a method to avoid creativity or find better ways to solve current problems, and then become stuck in the same pattern. Perhaps the most significant drawback from this approach is learning something from faulty assumptions, or even stop learning completely.

Fixed Mindset vs Growth Mindset

The combination is probably the most popular for its mental states. Simply put the term "fixed mindset" refers to one that is static in the sense that the belief is that you're competent at something, or not without any way to change this so-called "fact" or "destiny"..

However it is an approach to learning with an open-minded perspective. The mindset helps you be confident that you will be improved, change, and improve in any area by undergoing the correct education.

When you look back at the three perspectives, it's simple to recognize that each group permits you to discover the world, develop and become more satisfied in general. While the other one is the reverse.

Limiting beliefs may seem as a way to relax or be more easy to adhere to and less work, however they are costly. They not only block positive opportunities but also keep you in the way of achieving your maximum potential.

Chapter 2: Why Is Mindset Important?

Each mindset operates in a double way. As an example, although your own mindset could provide you with opportunities however, it could also set limits that are based on your assumptions and approaches in diverse situations.

As the way you think can aid in identifying potential opportunities, they could also be a trap for you to fall into self-defeating patterns too. The narratives you tell yourself as well as the thoughts you think about yourself could take a different direction.

If you find yourself in an unhelpful or restrictive mentality, then it is going to stop change from occurring throughout your life. However, if you cultivate positive mental attitudes then your abilities will grow.

Importance of Mindset In Life

As your mental state is a reflection of the beliefs you hold and beliefs, it is a powerful tool to impact the way you live. Most people's beliefs form the basis of their work. This is why beliefs differentiate the people who excel in their work and those that struggle constantly.

These assumptions form the base of your talents and where they originate. Consider your strengths as well as your intellect as well as your personal characteristics. Are you of the opinion that these qualities as permanently fixed and indefinite? Or do you feel they are qualities you can develop and build throughout your life?

Flexibility or rigidity of your beliefs determines the way you think.

Being in the right frame of mind for a specific task is almost an essential requirement to success. If you're a parent educator, student, business owner or working in a different occupation, you must have the correct mindset in order to succeed in what you do.

Every job comes with the challenges that come with it being positive will help you not only overcame those hurdles but also accept them as challenges and the chance to grow and develop.

When you examine the world around you will notice that individuals with similar situations have drastically different outcomes in their lives. It is due to their mental outlook.

Because your perspective on things and events affects your perception of these events it is possible that the outcome are different than those of those who is of a different mentality.

If you have an optimistic mindset and you'll be able to get over setbacks than those with a depressing or restrictive attitude. If you're a person with an unfavourable mindset it will feel like the whole world is about to slide away from you each time you encounter something unpleasant to experience.

If the beliefs you hold dear don't inspire you, it's likely that you're setting your self up for failure in a challenging scenario. There is a greater likelihood to giving up and accepting defeat when all you have to do is push to do better or maybe adopt an alternative approach. There is the possibility that you will need to alter your state of your mind.

Mindsets Are More Than Beliefs

Mindsets aren't just a set of thoughts and are able to determine your responses to various situations as well as other habits. They play a range of cognitive purposes and help you think about situations. In addition your mind will focus your attention on those most crucial signals, and eliminate irrelevant details so you don't overload your brain with too much information.

Your mental state can also provide you direction, by suggesting realistic goals you should achieve in order that you are aware of direction. As your thinking becomes routine is what defines your identity and the kind of person you could develop into.

Life Experiences Reinforce The Mindset

In the majority of cases the way they think is set by their parents at a young time. Perhaps it is through your teachers, parents, or other people that you easily learn from what is being taught.

When you're young, and without alternative source of information then you are able to accept this information. The information you receive is inside your mind and begins to form your views about the world and yourself in it.

As you age and become more mature Life experiences and life events might contradict the earlier information and alter your perspective. However, your earlier understanding persists and eventually becomes the basis for much of your existence. In the case of example, if your surroundings are filled with those who live constantly in a state of stress and anxiety, then you're likely to find that you'll have a mindset which mirrors the reactions of others by being anxious and stressed.

Your mental outlook continues to grow and grows stronger as you practice and repeat the beliefs you hold.

If you are caught within a negative, or even limiting attitude, then you'll probably be prone to self-talk that is negative and become aware of things a certain manner. It can turn into self-fulfilling until you believe that it's true.

The other side on the other hand, if are positive, you will be able to reinforce it through the beliefs you hold and your subsequent actions.

The Emotion Factor

But, it's not the only element that plays a role in the formation of belief systems and routines. Emotions also play a role into this mix. If you are mixing repetitive thoughts and actions emotion, the results you expect may change.

Good and bad routines are formed in the exact same method: through repetition. The habit is established more rapidly and more strongly when it is accompanied by emotional motivation.

Let's look at the instance of eating comfort food. It's clear that it's not healthy, but because it feels good during a time your mood is low You turn on this behavior to lift up your mood. When you are in the cycle, it becomes the habit of eating with a lot of emotional feelings and an unhealthy eating routine is created.

What Does Science Say About Mindsets?

Neuroscience, or the research into the nervous system reveals that our brains are constantly making and breaking down neural pathways. The pathways that are created, then create our thinking and behaviour patterns that tell the brain how to think or make decisions and to show you to the external world.

Of these, those that are utilized more frequently are stronger. Those who aren't used often end up becoming weak and are eventually removed.

The scientific evidence supports the reason for different mindsets due to the fact that our brains are wired with a desire to be able to absorb about new subjects. However there are that not learn and are trapped within a predetermined mindset.

Positive people have a higher likelihood of more likely to grow, as they believe that their capability can be improved. Contrarily those who have a negative outlook seem to be stagnant, which supports the idea that they are stuck at their current degree with little or no progress.

The two are the main areas important to us in this article and are referred to as the growth mindset as well as the fixed-minded. What differentiates them is that one concentrates on the outcomes attained, the other focuses on the method of doing it.

Fixed-minded people are focused on results like being hired for "that job" or losing "those 30 pounds" where one believes they're defined in terms of the results. A growth mindset believes that your effort in the process to achieve the desired result is much more important.

It is because you be more efficient, more imaginative, and effective by focusing on the process, not the end result. This leaves plenty of potential for growth and allows you to develop as an individual.

Moving forward, let's look at a look at every sort of.

Chapter 3: Fixed Vs Growth Mindset

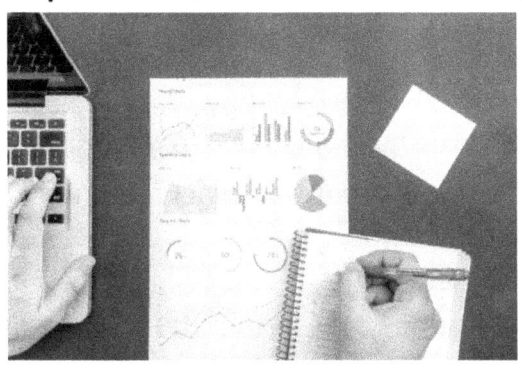

You've probably realized that how you view your abilities will have an influence on the outcomes you get in your the world. Incredibly, both mindsets, growth and fixed can be self-reinforcing but with radically different methods.

If you think that the aptitude is a ingrained or permanent feature that you are born with and isn't able to alter, then you have the fixed mentality. However, if you believe it is possible to develop this skill with effort and perseverance, you're in a growth mentality.

Every belief can lead to different actions and, consequently, diverse results. In both cases, being a person of growth, that is prepared and eager to grow and develop and grow, is essential to achievement.

But that isn't to say that effort perseverance, determination and effort aren't vital. They certainly are however only if your belief is that you're not limitless and in total charge of your own destiny.

Mindset in Practice

People with these mindsets do not just think differently, but also respond to information in an entirely different approach. The differences could be striking when you react to information regarding how they perform.

People who are fixed-minded react very positively to data regarding how they've completed some thing. It can be from making a fresh recipe or studying a new language and making a project of their own and achieving good marks at completing tests and grading. Their minds are the most engaged as they discover their achievements. Their primary, but less important concern is their performance, based and the praise they get.

However those who have a growth mindset are likely to respond best when given information on how they can enhance their performance. People with a growth mindset want to understand ways to improve themselves, that leaves plenty of potential for improvement.

They are interested in ways to assist them in their growth and to do that, rather than just their ability or talent.

Both are actually, very different strategies and the first one is centered around "How did I do?" in contrast to the latter, which focuses on "What can I do better next time?"

Fixed mindsets are all about how the result was seen and the growth mindset revolves around the ways to improve. It isn'thard to see whichmindset will yieldbetterresultsinthelong run.

Mindset In Action

In the case of making a decision, the fixed and the growth mindset are two different poles. For a famous example, let's consider an account of the tortoise and Hare.

In the tale, the horse was so confident that he would win, it sat down to sleep throughout the race. In contrast the tortoise kept going and believed it was in the best position of winning.

As the hare got up after waking up, he began running at the speed could.

However, he wasn't able to catch up. Meanwhile, the tortoise had already won.

The story demonstrates that the hare was of fixed beliefs and thought that his natural capability to run fast would ensure victory. The tortoise, however, had an evolving mindset, where he was convinced that he had to put in the effort until he reached a particular stage. However it was a man who wasn't afraid of failing, but was willing to face any task.

The same thing can be said about the possibility that a rigid mindset is susceptible to an unrealistically perfect perception of self-perception. Like the hare this type of thinking suggests your self-worth is already flawless. Your brain is less adept at recognizing potential to make improvements.

The Basics of Fixed vs Growth Mindset

People who have a fixed mentality take their characteristics as something that is expected. They think that they have an amount of ability and intellect and that nothing will alter that fact. Therefore, people who have this belief tend to be concerned about their talents and their abilities.

If you have a fixed mentality, you think that your capability is inherent and are apprehensive about failure because it forces you to question the level of excellence you actually have. A second belief held by those who are of this mind is that there's an upper limit of your potential.

In the case of instance, if you've had a difficult time in high school, you might feel that you're just not ready to go to college. It's possible that you won't even consider going to go to college, but end up trapped in a low-paying and boring job. This kind of job doesn't offer much to stimulate your mind and your belief in the lack of a place can become your reality.

However If you are a person with an attitude of growth, you are aware that you will increase your capabilities and failing is merely a reminder of what you need to be working on.

The people who are fixed in their attitude are focused on proving themselves. They often get defensive when someone points the fact that they committed mistakes. The fixed mindset allows them to judge themselves based on the mistakes they make.

The growing mindset in contrast, displays resilience and determination even in the face of failure. Instead of taking an approach of defense and focusing on their weaknesses, they are driven to improve their performance.

Check out the following statements about state of mind from people who have an innate and growing mindset:

Fixed-mindset Growth mindset

Math is a nightmare for me. Math is a challenge for me.

I'm not able to get to stay organized. I've tried to master organizing, but with no satisfaction.

I love cakes, but I'm not good at baking. I'd like to master baking, however I am not there yet.

It's not my forte to do origami. I'm still learning the art of origami.

It's evident in these instances that the quotes of the fixed-mind set tend to be more a declaration of resignedness, such as "horrible at", "can't seem to", "can't bake" as well as "no good at". It's a sign of a lack of willingness to attempt as if the individual thinks that the skills they possess do not belong to them. There is a sense of resoluteness in this class.

The group of people who are growth-minded provides examples that consist of more an observation rather than a claim. They suggest the possibilities to learn a new skill when someone puts in extra effort and strives to be better.

In order to distinguish the fixed mindset and the growth mentality, bear these things at the forefront:

Goals: The fixed mind is looking smart, whereas the growth mindset seeks to grow and develop.

Achieving challenges: The fixed mind avoids challenging situations, however the growth-oriented mind seeks out challenges.

Change: Change is viewed as a threat for people with fixed views, however those who are growth-oriented view it as a challenge.

Reaction to setbacks: People stuck in a fixed mentality are not able to handle setbacks well, seeming helpless. However, those with an optimistic mindset seem to be to be resilient.

Reaction to criticism: A rigid mindset can appear defensive when confronted with critique, but the growth mindset can learn from the experience.

Reaction to wrongdoing In response to wrongdoing, the fixed mentality tends to retaliate and punish when wrongdoing is committed, whereas the growth mindset prefers to compromise and educate.

The success of others A fixed mind sees the success of others as an obstacle, while those with a growth mindset view it as a source of inspiration.

Chapter 4: The Dangers Of A Fixed Mindset

The benefits of having a growth perspective may appear obvious however, many individuals have a preconceived notion of what they should do in particular scenarios. It can be extremely detrimental since this mentality blocks important capabilities from developing and advancing. It also affects the health and happiness of your family for the future.

In this case, we'll say that you're not an expert in science. If you constantly tell yourself that you're not an expert in science or science doesn't interest you

This becomes justification to stop studying the subject.

With a fixed-minded mentality, you can be able to avoid failure in the short-term, but it also limits your ability to develop as a person, to learn and develop new abilities in the long term.

However the person with a growing mindset may decide to try science even though they fail at the first. The person who is growing likely views failing as an indication to keep working to improve their abilities rather than admitting the fact that they're not good at what they do.

Over time the peer you are with will maximize their abilities as they decide to take advantage of criticism rather than ignoring it. They decide to take on an obstacle instead of trying to avoid this challenge and consider it an opportunity for learning instead of feeling intimidated.

Therefore, if you are thinking things such as "It's impossible to lose the weight", "I'm not a natural artist", "I'm not creative", or "I'm a procrastinator" then you'll be missing out on a lot of opportunities. When you finally stop learning, and don't grow more, and it gets difficult to become more proficient.

These are just a few of the things you're not aware of:

Undermining The Importance Of Effort

A fixed-minded mindset is one where essential qualities such as intelligence or talent are thought of as permanent traits. These people tend to record their talents or their intelligence, rather than improve these qualities. People may attribute their only their talent to achieve success with no efforts. If they're good at something, they readily attributing it to their abilities like scoring well on tests or working excellent on a task. Yet, at the when they think about it, they are also thinking of those skills that are less solid to be fixed. Instead of acquiring their skills, they take them for what they are without putting any effort into improvements, like "I'm not cut out to handle a paint brush".

They are content with as they are and they can't improve or even change.

The Obsession To Prove Worth

People who have a fixed mentality have a desire to demonstrate their worth. Each situation demands confirmation of their intelligence, personality or even their personality.

Each scenario is scrutinized, leading to questions such as "Will I succeed or fail?", "Will I look dumb or smart?", "Will I be rejected or accepted?" and on.

Even though they appear needing approval However, they're unlikely to do anything beyond what they can to get the results they desire so desperately. They are likely to be stuck due to their fear of rejection that they're unwilling to expand beyond their comfort zone.

The Desire To Be Flawless

Moving it up a notch The issue of a fixed mentality is that it's not enough to be successful, and neither is it enough to appear smart and skilled. The goal is to look pretty perfectly.

What happens at the end? Well, if your failure is a sign that you are not able or ability, you're stuck as an failure. It is impossible to move on beyond at this point.

In the end, you focus on not allowing failure to happen at any expense and attempting to keep your feelings of satisfaction. It is not a good idea to try something different because, if it doesn't believe you'll be successful at something, you don't like to be seen by others as someone who has witnessed your failure. The whole process could be extremely restrictive and stressful.

Decreasing Self-Knowledge

One among the worst consequences of having a fixed mind is the way it diminishes self-knowledge. Instead, the focus is shifted to external validations and rewards. This way of thinking, the focus can be diverted from internal advancement.

If you are constantly seeking public recognition and indicators of achievement, you can begin to fool not just others but also yourself. Also, it takes away what you are really.

The Need for Constant Validation

The way you think can impact the way you interact with other people. People who have a fixed mentality are anxious and expect their friends, partners as well as their peers to help them in any scenario.

They want to be with people who appreciate their abilities and boost their confidence levels. could not establish on their own. This can cause difficulties if relationship ends in a romantic way, or friends break up or a conflict develops between friends?

Each of these scenarios could cause a person to have an unchanging mindset, inadequate confidence, low self-esteem and lots of uncertainty and trepidation.

For a quick summary, here's what a fixed mind examines the world skills: A fixation on this as an inherent trait that isn't able to be modified.

Afflictions: The fixed mind considers this to be something you should stay clear of at all times. It is a constant threat that an obstacle could reveal the lack of ability and that you are prone to giving to the challenge in a hurry when you are in this situation.

The effort: It's considered unimportant by the mind of the established. This is something people turn to if they're not good enough for their task.

Feedback is a way to make those with a rigid mindset to go to be defensive. In the event of feedback, those in this type of mindset tend to view it as a personal attack and see it as an assault against their abilities or performance. If the feedback isn't the way they want it to be, they could decide to disregard the feedback altogether.

Resets: When confronted with backslides, those who have a rigid mindset tend to place blame on someone else. They can also be easily demotivated and tend to give up altogether.

Be aware that they are all causes that don't just create however, but can also reveal an unchanging mindset.

Moving from one mindset or the other is difficult, but it is doable. It is important to look out for triggers like these because the fixed mentality can be detrimental hinder your progress. Particular ways to break free from a fixed mentality could be outlined in the following ways:

Be aware of your own inner voice. If you do not and it isn't followed, it will dictate your actions in a routine manner, causing you to stay exactly where you are.

If you come across someone more skilled than you, take a lesson from their experience.

If you have to make a having to choose between something secure and challenging, you should go for the risk.

In the event that you experience an obstacle on the way consider what you can take away from the experience or how you could do to improve your situation.

If you are given feedback, do not be offended or interpret it personally. Find ways you can utilize this data to enhance the quality of your work.

Chapter 5: The Power Of A Growth Mindset

The growth mindset is a way for individuals to believe that they are adept even in every situation. They don't see that they are limited by their abilities at present however, they consider themselves capable of doing anything they wish provided they are able to practice.

Think about the scenario of receiving a brand fresh project which you've never previously worked on. Your response can go in any direction.

It's possible to take a look at the new challenges and feel that you're just not qualified for the job or think that these design, numbers or techs aren't for you. That would clearly reflect an uninformed mindset, and you'll not be able to take advantage of everything discussed in the earlier section.

But, it is also possible to take a look and begin to think about how you'll be able to make it work. It is possible to think about what you'll have in order to present your ideas as well as what you'd need to achieve the results you want. These qualities of optimism and imagination indicate the development of your mind, and will enable you to achieve these things:

Improvement Through Effort

Growth mindsets allow people to be convinced that the fundamental abilities of their brains are able to develop with hard work and commitment. To achieve this, abilities and minds are the initial steps and let the development of the foundations they have built.

These people display enthusiasm for learning as well as determination, which is essential to be successful. People who are a grower consider their strengths as qualities that can be developed by the dedication and work.

If you're a believer in growth, you're eager to experiment with different things since you realize that you can succeed only through the effort you put into it, not natural talent. It's not about the possibility of failure, because you are convinced that even if you fail, you'll improve and be successful with the future. Research suggests that people with a positive mindset are able to handle stress and pressure more effectively and result in higher health levels.

Offers A Sense Of Fulfilment

In contrast to the fixed-minded one of the primary advantages of a growth perspective is the many opportunities that can be seized. If you are a person who is growing that is constantly seeking improvement which is followed by the feeling satisfaction and fulfillment.

An appreciation for achievement can also be a signpost towards a higher level of quality. As you progress, you realize that being successful is a continual effort and not a quick fix.

Develops Resilience

Growth mindsets also help you improve your resilient. If you encounter challenges or setbacks, your mind is more optimistic in dealing with them.

If, for instance, you get feedback from your supervisor and you're aware that it's a useful learning technique which will assist you in setting proper goals and guidelines in the near future.

Buffers Against Demotivation

People who are driven by a desire to grow are always looking for new opportunities and challenges to be engaged instead of gaining satisfaction from the results. It means that they are driven to achieve ever more.

As a result of being more process oriented and not a solely result-oriented they excel when they are involved engaged in doing things. It is an opportunity to learn, it motivates them, and spurs people to work more.

In this case Instead of wanting an unfinished book that is perfect in its writing, the person with a growth mindset wants to attend to the continue to work on it continuously until it's done whatever it takes. Instead of focusing by a specific number on the scale, the growth mentality will be more focused on exercising every day in order to be more active and fit.

Encourages Perseverance

A growth mindset also demands perseverance. The goal of a growing mentality is not on the things that happen to you, but instead focus on what you can do for yourself.

Perseverance is also about kicking the fears of failure out of the window. That means taking risks whenever the opportunity arises and not limiting yourself to living an excessively preoccupied or anxious life.

The ability to persevere is a crucial element of a positive attitude. Since you won't achieve a 100% success in every task that you take on, having tenacity can allow you to reflect on your shortcomings correctly.

Inability to resolve the issue often opens the door to improve your abilities and to learn about something completely new. If you hit an obstacle, they tend to come up with an excuse or quit. A person who has the mindset of growth realizes the fact that failure is a necessary part of being successful.

In this way, they plan to fail mentally and are aware that failure will occur at one point or other. This doesn't scare the people they work with nor does it cause them to quit.

Furthermore, the ability to make mistakes reduces the stress from achieving a flawless result each time.

Promotes Critical Thinking

If you are talking about the process of learning, mistakes are essential because it requires the student to pinpoint where they committed a blunder. It also assists you to not just find the answer but also to develop an ability to make decisions.

Let's suppose you're asked an incredibly difficult question during class. If you turn off your brain when you're overwhelmed it won't help you grow or discover anything.

If you are able to recognize the issue by tackling at it continuously in asking questions and thinking carefully, you stand greater chances of getting answers. While doing this your effort exert will aid the brain to create new neural connections. It will also improve your ability to solve similar challenges. This is how you can get better and more proficient in everything you do.

Practice Makes Perfect

It is not a good idea to use an familiar cliche, but the practice of a growth mindset is indeed a way to become perfection, or perhaps more effective when it comes to what you are doing.

As the growth mind is driven more through a desire to learn instead of a longing for validation, practicing and hard work can foster qualities such as imagination and high-level of intelligence. The people who are in this mindset do not feel discouraged when they fail and do not see them as failing, but rather as growing.

It is true that repetition can play a crucial part in learning and is crucial to gain proficiency. The one thing most experts can agree on is the fact that practicing enhances the performance of your brain.

For a quick summary, a growing mentality sees these situations as follows: Skills: A growing mindset is based on the belief that capabilities are something that will always improve and improve. The ability to develop skills comes from working hard, and you shouldn't quit doing what you do.

Growth Mindset: A person who is a growth mind is eager to accept the challenges that come along and see them as opportunities to learn. Being able to take on challenges makes the mind more determined.

The ability to work hard is crucial to a positive mindset. It could even outweigh the ability. If the mindset of growth sees efforts as the way to success, it acknowledges that it is essential to continue studying.

Feedback A growth-oriented mindset considers feedback as a positive thing and a learning experience from. It's a good way to determine areas in need of improvements.

Settingbacks: Instead of placing the brakes on progress they are thought of as opportunities to increase the current skills and abilities.

Chapter 6: Can You Change Your Mindset?

It is possible to change your beliefs as they no longer benefit the person you are or allow you to reach your goal.

Resistant To Change

Though attitudes can shift however, it happens slow. Particularly if there are long-held beliefs regarding some thing. If, for instance, you've been taught that having an apple every day is healthy and you be hesitant to believe when someone else has told you the opposite.

While a preconceived mentality is simple to establish and maintain, it's a barrier to changing. For instance, consider an anchoring stake to keep an erect tent on the soil. Though it's possible to move it after it is put in place, it is difficult to take it off without a justification for doing so. When you've established a mental picture on something, it will affect the way you think about the subject. If, for instance, you find an event boring since the previous one that was of the same type was boring, you might decide not to attend in the first place. If you decide to visit and discover it not to be boring You may need an extended time to alter your perspective.

Using Fear To Change Your Mindset

Someone who has a preconceived notion tends to be more interested in appearing clever than trying new things. They do all they can to stay out of humiliation and will ignore the things they are actually lacking in. That is they are afraid of appearing foolish.

It's an inhibitory aspect. There is a chance that this is a result of a sense of rejection or denigration in childhood or from events kept in your mind, which you might not recall consciously.

Due to this fear of the unknown Your fixed mentality is one that avoids new experiences and stifles learning. This slows your growth and can lead you to behave in a lazy manner.

In order to combat this and to change your mind You must be conscious of the fear that drives your actions. You must then recognize that this anxiety is not rooted in your current reality. The only way to defeat it is to get over the fear and let it go.

For instance, those with fixed views view their level of intelligence as fixed. They are primarily concerned with showing that they're intelligent and hiding the fact the fact that they're not.

In this way, they are prone to stay clear of situations in which they may fall short. They are also not able to recover from defeats and would rather doing tasks that they already excel at.

It is the same for other people with this attitude who limit their efforts and undermine their work.

Using Actions To Change Your Mindset

A different approach to transforming mindsets is to take action since abilities and abilities are developed through repeated practice and repetition. A key element to transforming the mindset of a fixed one is to recognize and disproving the fixed mental voice, and then taking growth-oriented actions frequently.

Even though this rarely occurs overnight, it is possible to build new abilities through deliberate repetition and training. With each new skill you learn the voice of your fixed-mind decreases.

Identifying Your Counter Mindsets

The mindsets are formed by previous experiences as well as emotional milestones. However, when they don't produce the outcomes you expected, they are rebranded as contrary mental models.

It can lead to thoughts of self-doubt and doubt, negative opinions and negative thoughts that stand out of the way of making the process of growth. In the majority of cases this negative thought pattern occurs in such a way that you may not be aware of they are there.

Consider that nagging voice that makes snide remarks while you're looking at yourself in the mirror. This is the voice that makes you feel unsatisfied with how you appear, and makes you hesitant in introducing yourself to someone new, or even if you wish to think about a change in career.

Everybody is experiencing negative thoughts or thoughts to some degree however the harm is in the collateral. This can cause you to regularly ruin your hopes and dreams, making difficult to stay optimistic. All that is left are the nagging reminders of "I can't talk to him/her", "I'm not smart enough for that", "I'm not qualified enough" or "I'm out of shape" and the like.

In order to change your perspective You must be aware of when that voice is raised, and also the frequency at which it occurs. This will help you determine the reasons behind your opposing mindset, and then narrow it down to a handful of key issues.

Shifting Gears From The Negative To The Positive

After you've established the negative thoughts, you must be able to keep these thoughts from hindering your progress. When a negative thought comes to mind you can counter it with immediate, but positive response.

Imagine you'd like to take a stroll at the end of dinner, to engage in an physical activity. However, the issue is that after dinner, you hear telling you that you're exhausted and full or it's just too late for you to leave right now.

You can stop this pattern of thinking right now when you get up and put on your shoes for walking.

In most cases, the initial step can get rid of that annoying sounding voice inside your head.

Understand "WHY" You Need To Change

Change in mindset takes an enormous amount of determination and dedication as established patterns are difficult to change. The challenge is made even harder as a large portion of your harmful or restricting habits established when you were young and you've continued to do exactly the same things from the beginning.

Knowing why you should modify a behavior or mindset makes it easier to make it meaningful. Two things will be helpful: motivation and determination.

The first step is to depend on your motivational skills to help you change the way you live, and although you'll find that the "why" will provide you with the motivation you need, it could be difficult to sustain over the long term. That's where your willpower needs to come in to help maintain your motivation.

The problem is that willpower could get a bit shaky quite fast. Consider trying to eat better and you come across an assortment of Girl Scout cookies next to the bowl of fruit at work. Perhaps you can get your resolve to resist eating the biscuits.

Then, you're planning for a workout at the end of your shift, but you have to leave for a reason. When you're finished and exhausted, you're not just tired but fumbling for willpower also. And, of course, the fact that you were unable to keep to the plan you had originally set will not help.

What happens if you are doing the gym, or heading straight to home? It's likely that you know since it is the same for everyone.

If you attempt to make changes in your lifestyle the power of motivation and determination on their own, they might not be sufficient by themselves. This is why many give up altering their behavior shortly after they've started, inability to keep their commitment.

What you should do is be more forgiving, and give your self some time to allow to stumbles and mistakes. An unchanging mindset is not a good thing.

You are emotionally exhausted and uneasy to experiment with something new.

Start Small To Finish Big

One of the most effective strategies to shift your thinking is to take small steps to reach your goals. The quest to be more healthy, prosperous or intelligent as well as being more peaceful, compassionate and more successful will never be simple. You must combat all the demons that have been ingrained into your mind from the earlier years.

If you are overwhelmed most of the time Try to sit at least two minutes each the night prior to sitting in a lotus posture for an uninterrupted half-hour and with a running mind.

If you'd like to get fitter Start by doing the one-time push-up. Increase your strength along with your attitude until you reach a formidable number of 20.

Set a small goal and work towards it with a positive attitude. In the majority of cases, you'll discover that you do more than what you intended to achieve (maybe up to three push-ups instead) and feel happy when you exceed your goals. Other days, you could just do the minimum, and still feel great knowing you have achieved the objective. A lot of people feel it's useless to begin with a small amount, but consistently achieving tiny goals with success can allow you to create new mental habits.

Chapter 7: Strategies To Develop A Growth Mindset

If you let your results, like your exam results, weight, job, or even your physical appearance determine you You become a subject to a fixed mentality. Contrarily the growth mindset is about learning. You are able to speed up your learning with these well-tested and proven methods.

Continual Learning

The growth mindset is all about growing and evolving. In other words, instead of looking for approval from other people You should connect with others who will help you grow.

It means you won't have to justify every single thing you perform. This will only mean you're not able to achieve your goals to grow. Be sure to prioritize learning prior to approval, as it can help you develop and be successful in your endeavors.

In the same way exploring new ideas helps to come up with new concepts and help you become conscious of the skills you're proficient in. Also, you can challenge you with different tasks in order to increase your abilities.

Be Committed

If you combine continuous learning with a commitment to learning to your goals, you are setting yourself up for success.

A lot of individuals make the error of a shaky commitment and believe that they're committed to their purpose or cause and yet they're actually not. In a state of uncertainty the people decide to test things, and let it go and wait to discover the results.

When they are working, many tend to focus only on the fact that they've not reached their objective yet, and cannot stop considering how far they'll need to travel. A negative mindset could impede your goals, making you more inclined to quit.

If you can develop the mindset of growth the problem is eliminated. If you make the decision you're fully dedicated to reaching your objectives, regardless of the obstacles, you're much more likely to be successful.

Here'saverysimple, everydayexample. When you wake up, you jump from bed anxious that you'll be late for the bus or carpool. You do not eat breakfast, get dressed quickly and leave the house but only to discover you've actually been late for your bus. The person with a fixated mindset is likely to react by murmuring and cursing and will remain in a negative attitude for the remainder of the day.

However, if you're striving to build a business and you consider this an opportunity to begin regularity so the same thing doesn't happen.

Your response will be getting up early to sleep by setting a alarm, and then laying out your outfit at night, so the next day is more pleasant and more unique.

You don't have to plan it in your mind, but take the initiative to implement it through.

Develop Healthy Self Esteem

It is very difficult to strive for or reach achievement without self-confidence. To be able to improve or grow it is essential to be confident that you're competent to achieve your goals. Because you don't have the money to let yourself down It is crucial that you don't worry about the opinions of others.

Your self-esteem reflects how you perceive yourself as an expression of the way you think. It's a result of the internal dialog that you have with yourself in which you judge and judge your value, whether positive or not.

In order to have confidence in yourself You need to have a solid mental attitude, one that permits you to change and develop.

Work On Your Perspective

Each mindset is connected with the concept of perspective. Your beliefs, ideas of bias, attitudes and beliefs can affect how you think about information and perceive your surroundings. A growth-oriented mindset can increase chances of developing an optimistic outlook and getting the long-term success you want to achieve.

The perspective is also the primary factor in motivating. Motivation will determine whether you're in a position to meet your objectives over the long term. It acts as motivational factor to help you keep going until you cross the end of your road. If you are not motivated, you'll get discouraged when confronted to challenges. One of the best ways to ensure that you are motivated is to think about your "WHY why'. Why did you get started? What is the reason it's important for you?

In the case of need to lose weight do you think it's because you are unhappy with how you're feeling about your current condition or does it happen just because you want to look and feel better? If either one of them will propel toward your goals however, one that is triggered by feelings of being deficient could seem more elusive.

Set Effective Goals

Many factors can influence a person's development mental outlook. The most important of these is the making sure that you set goals that are meaningful and achievable.

If goals are set in a realistic manner and realistically, they are more likely to be able to meet these goals. Attaining major goals or small milestones toward a larger target is an effective development process that helps to develop the attitude.

The mind of a resilient person can get you through rough times and assist you get ready for your next adventure.

Manage Your Inner Negative Voice

One of the greatest obstacles in achieving a positive mindset is that you have a voice in your head. The voice that keeps on insisting that you cannot achieve it and it's not worth the effort, but that you're who you are and it's time to accept that.

The inner voice echoes the belief that all things are granted and you only have limited control over the course of your life. All people, not just those who have the growth mindset, have this voice. To change your perspective, you must be able to control this voice.

To begin, turn your "can't" in your mind to "can" and add a "yet" to the end of your sentences.

Facing Adversity

The growth mindset can be adept at overcoming obstacles. If you are looking to make it through rough times it is essential to take on each challenge with determination.

If you don't face challenges then you won't be able to fully realize the potential you have or acquire new capabilities. The challenges you face can be an opportunity to grow and learn so that you develop as well.

People who have a mindset of growth thrive in the face of challenges that help them to move ahead.

Be Open To Feedback

An optimistic mindset is always open to feedback since it's a chance to improve. Feedback can also be a chance to increase your efficiency. It allows you to determine the areas require improvement and also where you're excelling.

As feedback is offered by other people, it's essential to communicate with people. Engaging in networking or socializing could require getting out of your comfortable area to stimulate your creativity.

Imagine a situation in your workplace where the boss contacts you to discuss a report you've put together or a task you're managing. In a preoccupied mentality, you'll see the situation as an opportunity to slap yourself. It is also possible to end up thinking that you're not enough for the job or your boss has no clue as how for the job to be done.

If you're lucky it's likely that your day will be spent on talking about and criticizing and, even, in the worst-case scenario you may even be job-hunting. If you work to cultivate a mindset of growth, it will be easier to see the same situation as a valuable learning event. It will be easier to assess your work and get constructive feedback which will help determine how you can enhance your work. Instead of murmuring and grumbling it will be more straightforward.

Chapter 8: How To Deal With Setbacks

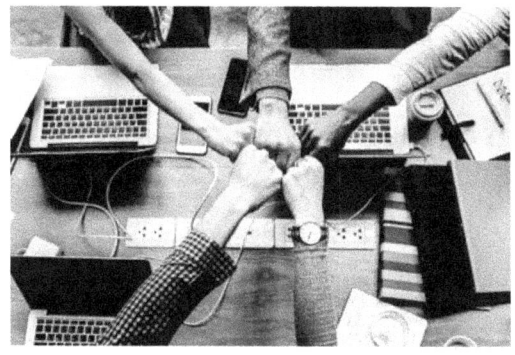

When you've discussed the good and bad aspects of different perspectives, it becomes apparent that the manner in which your mind reacts to failure, disappointment, or even failures is crucial.

In the case of people with fixed views, any setback can be seen as an event that alters the reality. The distorted perspective blocks people from seeing the situation as what it really is. If there isn't a clear view of the problem the situation can be difficult to change direction, resolve or even make progress.

However, for those who have a growth-oriented perspective, this loss doesn't get excessive. It's typically viewed as a factor which can help you redirect your energy to the right direction.

The Importance Of Failure

For those who want to be successful, failure can be a chance to learn the differences between what they were hoping for and what they achieved.

Anyone who is interested in improving the performance of their team and achieving better results to the next level A small setback could be a significant step towards success. The reason is that a delay gives you the opportunity to pinpoint the root of the issue and adjust your future actions to address the issue.

Because it is essential to recognize that there can not be any situation in which all is flawless It is also important to be prepared for setbacks along the road.

The mindset of growth sees the failure as a way where it will be able to gain important life lessons:

Experience And Knowledge

The most important thing you can learn after a setback or failure is through learning from experience. When you commit a blunder it is a the experience of a firsthand person, which will help you to gain a better comprehension.

This can change the way you think and begin to reflect on the reality of the world.

Another benefit of this is that it provides with its firsthand knowledge. If you are a growth-minded person then you can use this information in the future to avoid that identical failing.

Resilience And Growth

Resilience is also built through setbacks. For success, it's essential to know how to stay resilient. So that the first impulse you have is not to stop.

This same determination can lead to growth when you develop even in the face of challenges. Knowing that it's normal to have a setback every now and then will allow you to bounce back from failure more quickly.

While failure is acceptable however, it's never okay to quit.

Change Your Strategy

A failure is a great means of recognizing the need to change the strategies or plans you have in place. It is crucial to create a solid idea of what you want to achieve however, the plan should not be a fixed plan.

It should also be flexible enough to permit the possibility of reviewing your plan by adjusting, measuring and reevaluating things while you progress. One important thing to remember when it comes to this is that the goals you set remain the same, but your strategy should always evolve.

Seeking Inspiration Through Others

As you've already observed this, the growth mind seeks motivation from other people who have succeeded in something, are more effective and achieve the results you want.

If you start to look at celebrities from different walks of life, and you'll see that each successful individual has had a few challenges before they achieved success.

Using Failure As Leverage

Setbacks can be used to leverage your position and not just get back from it, but also accelerate forward. In order to leverage the setbacks you have, you must know the areas you fell short and the reasons for it. Also, you must know the things you could do better as well as how you can avoid making repeating the same mistakes.

It will assist you in learning to overcome your failures instead of thinking failure is the complete loss. By focusing on the right way, you can develop and grow, gain insights and perspectives about everything from love, business, life as well as relationships and individuals.

Through this process, you'll be required to create new connections, and bridge the gap where you couldn't join to the dots prior.

Redefining Priorities And Values

Based on the way you think Setbacks may either help the difference or ruin you. In the case of a growth mindset failing can help you reconsider the priorities you have set.

If you recognize that setbacks are only an obstacle for a short time You begin to think over it. It is time to reorganize the those things you consider most crucial and move other things around. To try to recover and make improvements then you begin making necessary adjustments. While doing so every failure can help to redefine your values. Because the mindset of growth is based around constant improvement and growth it is possible to see the values you had ten years ago before may not be your current value.

It's an ongoing work in advancement that allows you to keep moving forward, leaving behind setbacks.

Don't Let Your Failure Define You

In the event of an obstacle, you may be tempted to allow it to shape your perception of yourself. A broken-up relationship could cause you to believe you're not as attractive as you thought. A job you really wanted, but couldn't find, might convince you that you're not very smart at all.

It's crucial to recognize that the value you bring can't be determined solely by circumstances. The best option is to determine your talents and capabilities by examining important setbacks that you've experienced in the recent past.

Analyzing how you have overcome the obstacles you faced earlier can help to develop a strategy.

Helps Reach Your Potential

In the majority of cases, failure signifies that they have attempted. They have put in the effort in order to accomplish something, but it failed to produce results. Both failing and attempting could be valuable to anyone who has a growing perspective. The failures can improve your thinking skills and allows you to increase the potential of your future endeavors.

This builds your confidence in ways that you didn't think possible, by making you accountable of your errors. Sometimes, it's difficult to recognize the potential you have until you've overcome failure. It also aids in figuring out your abilities.

Failure Is Always Better Than Regret

A failure is an excellent option to not regretting. Imagine living with regret and not knowing exactly what would have been the outcome if you had been able to get that job. Compare it to having failed to land the position, but then finding out what your weaknesses are. If you fail, at least with the choice, you'll be more likely to get this right next time around.

Achieving success that is easy can creates a lot of space to fail, since it can make you believe you are in control and nothing can be wrong. Failure can teach you to not to underestimate your success and work more hard the next time. However, regret contrary to what you think does not provide the same opportunity and leaves you feeling miserable.

Setbacks Yield A Sense Of Direction

A lot of people think twice about their decisions. It's not because they are either right or wrong, but because they're not sure of what the outcome will be.

However, if a decision suffers the wrong way, it will point towards a way to redirect. The growth mentality is quick to seize this chance and gain knowledge from its failures. This helps you gain the exact location of what have gone wrong, and then how you can make changes to rectify your mistake.

In addition, since redirection can take the user to new places it allows you to discover new possibilities and break away from your normal routine. This is why failure could also assist you in getting out of the terror of taking a step outside of your comfort zone.

Chapter 9: The Science Of Growth Mindset

There is a common misconception that the mindset theory is simply a notion. Since everyone wants to learn help themselves and find topics that will aid them in improving their own lives, many get lost amid all of the various bits of information available. It has led to many individuals not having an accurate concept of what it is that truly defines growth mindset or the evidence that there is a real existence. A lot of people don't believe there is any evidence in it, based on an abundance of false information that's mixed up with actual factual information.

It is a good thing that it is true that mental health has extremely strong scientific foundations, which you could use as proof that whatever that you put into your mental state can be extremely beneficial to the ability of you to develop the mindset of growth. This section will discuss the scientific basis of the growth mindset and explain the reasons why it is important to your life.

Theory Founder

The concept of the growth mindset was formulated around thirty years ago by a woman who was Carol Dweck. Together with her coworkers, they were interested in understanding the attitudes of their students around"failure. "failure." They developed the interest following two different responses towards failure among their students Some bounced back and felt motivated to be better while others were devastated, no whatever the mistake was believed as.

Fixed Mindset VS. Growth Mindset

After conducting numerous studies that involved hundreds of students, Carol Dweck coined two terms which are fixed mindset and the growth mental state. The terms define the fundamental beliefs of each individual regarding intelligence and learning. People who think they are able to improve their intelligence and recognize that it requires work and dedication to grow more proficient in their abilities are thought to possess an "growth mindset." They are more likely to be driven to be more efficient as they enjoy the challenging classes that allow them to grow and they are keen on increasing their level of intelligence. They do not think they possess a fixed degree of intelligence but rather, they believe they can alter and improve their abilities as they progress through the years, thanks to practicing. In the end, they're more likely to put themselves into practice as well, and continue to learn that leads to them possessing a higher level of levels of intelligence.

A different approach to growth is fixed-minded. Like you would expect, this mindset is in complete contrast to the growth mentality. The people who are stuck in a mentality believe they are at the same degree of intelligence that can't be altered, regardless of what they do. They're less inclined to try new skills since they don't believe they are capable of doing so, and feel intimidated by challenges. They want things that are easy to do and prefer to get everything completed perfectly. The people who are fixed tend to believe that small failures are a negative impression of their character as a person, and are very disappointed. It is possible that they are drawn to doing what that they're already proficient at and avoid learning something new.

Neuroscientific Discoveries

Recently, there has discovered neuroscientific findings that confirm Carol

Dweck and her colleague's hypothesis. Scientists from the field of neuroscience have found they can see that our brain is more flexible than we had previously believed and have discovered directly linked events and the connectivity between neurons. When a person does something different, the neural networks that are already in place create by creating new connections. They also reinforce existing networks and create a protective layer around connections that are accountable for speeding up the transfer of impulses.

What it means the basic idea is that the more you do things, the more your brain develops. It not only grows in order to take on learning and new skills however, it also builds the ones you already have. When you are constantly practicing learning new skills, the more healthy your brain's capability to build new neural pathways, and the more a breeze it will be for you to master more about new subjects in the near future.

There are a few "good habits" that can be cultivated, that will help enhance these neural pathways as well as build upon the ones already in place. Activities like practicing doing exercises, asking questions, or eating healthy meals and enough rest help you to build a stronger brain with a more positive development mindset.

The Value of Growth Mindset

As well as neuroscientific breakthroughs, other researchers began to learn more about the growth mind-sets also. Researchers discovered that there's an incredibly strong connection between mental attitude and success. That is that If you believe that you are capable, then you will. If you believe you cannot, you cannot.

The people who believe that they can discover new skills, their minds can expand, or whatever they wish to do often are able. They come up with a method which, in turn that happens. Conversely, those who don't believe that they have the ability, are unable to. It is due to a preconceived notion of success and less satisfaction and motivation.

There is no doubt how important it is that people invest in growing their minds so they are able to achieve everything they wish to accomplish. If they are looking to boost their earnings, develop new abilities, boost the capacity of their brains or do anything else that requires a growth mentality will most likely attain it in some way. If they don't, they have a growth mindset will never be able to achieve the goals they would like to attain in their life.

When Does Growth Mindset Benefit You?

The growth mindset is beneficial in a variety of ways. It is possible to accomplish whatever you put your mind about doing with a positive mentality. Based on the idea that you are convinced you will help you make things occur. It is possible to learn how to boost the value of your money, master new abilities, acquire different languages, increase your vocabulary, pursue new interests, boost the physical health of your body, boost the activity of your brain, among other things, when you develop a growth attitude.

How Do You Get a Growth Mindset?

Whatever attitude you are currently in fixed, growth or fixed mind-set, you are able to shift to the mindset of a growing one. To develop an attitude of growth requires time and effort and dedication, but with the right implementation of strategies, sufficient patience and time, as well as sufficient effort, it is possible to achieve a growing mindset. In this book, you will be taught the exact steps to develop your own growth mindset and also how to keep it going. This is precisely what the book was designed to help you do!

A mindset that is focused on growth can be a potent attitude and a strategy which can help you achieve nearly anything you wish to accomplish in your daily life. A lot of people profit from a growth mentality, regardless of the age they were at in their lives in the moment they began developing one. If you've been a believer in growth for a long time, or are beginning to develop one as you age it is still possible to benefit from a growth mindset. There is no time to lose to discover the benefits of the growth mindset and the ways you can apply it to improve your quality of life. You can also live your most fulfilling life.

Chapter 10: Truth Behind Growth Mindset

The growth mindset is an extremely beneficial tool utilized to aid individuals with achieving greater benefits in their pursuit of individual growth. Like you learned in the last section, there are a lot of misperceptions surrounding growing mind-sets. We will focus our attention on the truth about this mentality. The growth mindset is an important ability that aids numerous people to achieve better success from whatever they wish to do, whether it being learning new techniques or learning new languages or accomplishing anything else they wish to achieve. This section will assist you to determine the reality of growing mindset as well as the distinctions between optimism and growth mindset or any other mental practices and actions.

Misconceptions

One of the main misconceptions regarding growth mentality is that it's an identical thing to being flexible and open with your ideas. That isn't the case. Being positive, open and able to change your opinions is usually believed to be what growing mindsets are, however this actually is referred to as "false growth mindset" in the world of research. It is basically individuals who possess the "I already have it, and I always have" mentality. The reason for this is they believe in a certain belief about their level of intelligence this is the definition of a fixed mind. They are unable to foster the growth of their brains, and so they fool their minds by presenting these views as the chance to think that they're developing, but actually, they're not.

Be open to different people's views and beliefs can be great, however it doesn't mean you're actually taking any classes. In addition, there's nothing you can do to have a completely growth-oriented mind. This is almost impossible because we're all stuck to some degree or other. It is essential to recognize this and accept this, but still strive to be able to progress in some way. It is the only way to cultivate the most growth mentality as is humanly feasible, and gain the rewards you want out of it.

Another myth is that the it is all about the praise of others and rewarding efforts. Ineffective efforts focused on the rewards or result isn't considered as growth mentality. It is more of an effort made solely for the rewards when it is over. True growth-oriented mindset does not have anything related to outcomes or rewards, instead it's built on the growth and learning process. If you're committed to the growth mindset and you're invested in this process, regardless of result. Although you might be able to imagine or hope of what you want to achieve however, that is not the point of working. You are instead determined to understand the procedure, and desire to remember all the information that you can.

Teachers as well as bosses try to utilize the growth mindset to reward their workers or students with rewards after a job accomplished. If their employees or students don't have a growing mindset, they perform in a way that is hardly motivating or energy. The motivation they have comes from the rewards themselves, rather than the process of learning. Even though this could inspire them to complete their tasks accomplished, it hasn't been able to inspire them to cultivate the mindset of growing.

In the end, determining your the process of developing a mindset can be a lot more difficult as "just do it." It is not enough to "have" a growth mindset. You must want it and then be willing to be a part of it. If you're not doing this then you won't be able to develop a attitude. A growth mindset stems from having the motivation to work hard and perform well. If you're not driven to work, it will be difficult for you to focus and be successful. It is possible to accomplish things however, you won't succeed in learning something. It is not enough to "have" a growth mindset and expect to have it, and put money into developing one. It's something that must be worked for regularly otherwise, you'll not ever have it.

Positivity VS. Optimism

For a deeper understanding of the concept of growth mindset crucial to look at the distinction between positivity and optimism. While they might sound identical to one another however, there are some significant differences between them. Learning these distinctions will enable you comprehend what it means to remain optimistic rather than optimistic.

The act of having a positive attitude. It is the way that it can be taught will require you to avoid all unpleasant, unsettling or in any way detrimental towards your ultimate objective. Instead, concentrate on only the good aspects and leave the rest "work itself out."

The same is true for optimism, but it allows you to see negativity. You can tackle it, be a part of it and progress throughout your day, embracing both all the positives and bad things. However, the benefit of this is the fact that you decide to find the positive aspects within your life. Although you might be dealing with and overcoming bad aspects, you're prepared to embrace those parts and take lessons from the experience. They are seen as an advantage by allowing these to serve as lessons and ways to move ahead, not barriers and excuses that keep your back.

When you're trying to cultivate the growth mindset and a growth mindset, it's important that you do not try to become a person who is only positive that is incapable of recognizing their own reality. It isn't beneficial and will not benefit your growth in any way or way. If you are truly determined to develop a mentality, you'll cultivate the belief that you can succeed. It is possible to embrace those difficult as well as the "bad" parts of life and utilize them as an opportunity to grow in order to do better. What is important is to use your opportunity to gain knowledge. Be aware that the growth mindset concentrates on the process of learning as well as the ability of one to keep studying. If you aren't embracing this concept, you will have need to work hard to develop the true growing mentality. The key is to recognize how to differentiate between these two and decide to choose positivity over optimism.

True Growth Mindset

Although positive attitudes as well as open-mindedness, and rewarding you and your coworkers with a well-done job are all good qualities but they don't encompass what a true growth mindset truly.

In simple terms, growth mindset is the mental state that goes along with the process of growth within our brains. This is the mentality people have when they believe we have the ability to do something and so can. It is this mindset that must be in place to be able to engage in activities and encounters that help our minds to grow within our brains. It is this activity that initiates the development of our brains, the reinforcement and the stimulation of our neural pathways. This happens when we acquire new abilities, increase the capabilities of our existing abilities as well as engage in activities and learning.

This isn't something that we are able to "have," but rather it's something we strive toward. This isn't something that we are able to achieve and be able to keep. It is an ongoing maintenance procedure which is a constant effort to achieve balance in the course of time. The growth mindset is not something you can easily attain. We must be driven by which is why we put our money into it. It is not possible to continue with inactive and sluggish actions, and label it a growth mindset, since there is no progress. Only in the context of a committed, motivated as well as productive mental strategies as well as actions that contribute to an increase in the neural pathways within our brains.

Learning the facts about the growth mindset and what exactly constitutes growing mindset will allow you to know the ways this ability can benefit your everyday life. Though you could certainly decide to create a false impression of growth if you want, be aware that it is not a real benefit to you or your brain, and could cause you to not gain any benefits for the efforts you have put to your own personal development. True growth-oriented mindset requires work to engage, invest, and the desire to achieve. However, even if you do that, you will not truly achieve it. You will instead striving to achieve it with continuous effort to build your ability to have an optimistic mindset.

Chapter 11: Benefits Of Growth Mindset

It is well-known that growing mindsets can bring numerous benefits to your everyday life. It can help you get your desired salary as well as helping you to learn techniques and many other aspects, growth mindset could assist a great deal. But, there are additional benefits to a growing mindset that aren't often thought of. Understanding these benefits will assist you to understand the goals you're working on as well as inspire you to keep working on your own growth mindset. Numerous benefits accrue from a growth mindset. So make sure you be patient and learn precisely what these benefits are and the implications for your life.

Enjoy Life More

One of the most important benefits of a growth mind is learning to appreciate life more. People with a fixed mentality are often anxious and be driven to excel at all things. This is why they are more likely to avoid trying new skills and putting themselves to the test because they avoid failure as well as the anxiety caused by failing.

People who are a believer in growth don't worry about becoming poor at something since they consider it an opportunity to improve. As they possess a positive view of the process of learning and do not suffer from the effects of perfectionionism as well as the anxiety that goes from it, they are able to more easily enjoy their lives. They're not afraid of learning new techniques or experiment with something new because they're no longer afraid to be "bad" at it. They realize that everybody starts somewhere and they're willing to begin with whatever level they're at. They are not afflicted by the pressure to excel at all things, and so they're prepared to make mistakes until they master it.

Improved Self-Esteem and Self-Confidence

If people are prone to a fixed mentality, they be prone to struggling with perfection. They fear doing things wrong as they feel humiliated and feel like being a failure due to it. People with the mindset of growth can see the fact that perfectionists are not necessary and that it is okay to fail. They consider everything an opportunity to improve and improve, consequently, they don't spend all their time being embarrassed or ashamed of doing things incorrectly. Instead, they recognize that they're simply taking their time learning. This eases anxiety and stress associated with perfectionists and makes people more likely to experience confidence in themselves and have self-confidence.

Ability to Forgive

People who are in an open-minded mindset will be able to recognize the fact that everyone, even themselves have mistakes. Therefore, they're more adept at accepting the fact that they and others are guilty who make mistakes. They view these mistakes as an opportunity to improve and become better at what they do, thus they do not worry over the errors that happen. They are not quick to criticize themselves or other people for being "silly" or "embarrassing themselves" in the process of learning new skills or doing something that they're not skilled in. Instead, they're willing to accept errors, and forgive the same way.

Realistic Perception of Reality

The people who are stuck in a mentality and are plagued by perfectionists and being unable to admit mistakes are likely to think that they live in a world where humans will never make a mistake. It puts lots of pressure on them. It also result in an untrue perception of the world. They think they need to have superhuman abilities to be loved and accepted by their world and real world.

The people who live with an open-minded mindset realize that humans make mistakes, and there's nothing they can do about the fact that they make mistakes. This means that they're more inclined to accept the reality of life and continue to live their lives as they should. They're less likely take on all the stress and pressure of being flawless, instead, they're open to mistakes and lessons. They are aware that no one wants to be perfect, consequently, they are free from these expectations and pressures.

Increased Resilience

Again, the absence of pressure to achieve perfection means that those with growing mindsets can reap the benefits of a growth mindset. They have greater levels of resiliency because they are not under pressure to achieve perfection. This means that they can make mistakes, forget about it, and come back. These are the people who will be more likely to persevere with even though they aren't proficient at it right at the beginning. They're willing to try as they make mistakes and admit their mistakes. At the end of the day, they tend to be better at learning since they don't abandon their new technique out of fear of losing or appearing foolish.

Regard Setbacks as Useful Lessons

The people who are fixed in their attitude view failures, setbacks, or even setbacks as obstacles unachievable. They fear that they get themselves into trouble to the point of getting stuck between these barriers. They shun these challenges. People who are a an attitude of growth consider these challenges as learning opportunities. They're keen to learn ways to overcome the obstacles to come out from the other end stronger than before. They're more likely look at setbacks, mistakes, challenges, and other obstacles throughout their lives as lessons instead of as a barrier.

Finding Joy in Processes

The people who have a growth mentality are truly happy discovering the process of life and adapting to the new circumstances and difficulties. They're interested in learning the ways to improve and are able to fully engage and become involved in the process of learning. They consider everything from determination of their goal, through the action taken, and the remuneration as equally rewarding.

The people who have a fixed mind tend to focus more on reward and goal but often do not achieve their goals because they're not willing to perform the tasks required for achieving the objectives. They fear making mistakes, and tend to be afraid of failure. They don't invest their time or get involved in the process and do not discover anything new or make accomplishments nearly as often as people with a growth attitude.

There are a myriad of beneficial and powerful advantages to growing your mindset. It not only helps to increase the number of neural pathways and networks however it helps living a life which is truly happier and healthier. It also makes your life more enjoyable. If you cultivate the growth mindset and continue to strive to achieve that goal, you're more likely to experience fulfillment within your daily life, and also your life will be more likely to be fulfilling. You are less likely to experience being depressed, experiencing excessive stress levels as well as perfectionism and other negative beliefs or conditions since you're not restricting your self-esteem through a fixed mental model.

Chapter 12: Transforming Your Mindset

Prior to establishing your own growth mindset it is essential to prepare to change your thinking. Dweck was the eminent founder of the concept of growth mindset declared that there are three "stages" for people: fixed mindset, transition and a growth mentality. In order to truly adopt the mindset of growth it is necessary to go through the phase of transition.

The transformational portion of the process will require the focus to be more on the identification of your mental patterns rather than dealing by implementing specific changes in your behavior. Before making specific changes, you must determine the things that need to change. It is possible to do this by observing your progress and knowing where your fixed perspective is within your daily life and the ways you are able to pinpoint the issue. The process takes some amount of time, and so it is important to take your time and be mindful when dealing with it.

When you're in the process of transformation There is one aspect you should be aware of that your limiting mindset has a deeper root than what it seems at a superficial level. You are likely to have something in your life that led you to this book, but how much you are paying attention to your surroundings, the more you're likely to observe your rigid mentality and the ways that it has established it in your daily living. Because this could be your first time really committing to the growth perspective, you've probably maintained a fixed outlook throughout your life. That means the signs could be a lot more deeply than you think they'll do. It's crucial to take your time when you are doing this and make sure be patient with the process. If you are able to identify your mindset that is fixed to be successful, the better chance will come from changing your thinking to an evolving mentality.

Your Fixed Mindset Has a "Voice," Listen to It

You may be surprised to learn that your fixed mentality is actually an "voice." This voice is one that tries to convince you that there's nothing to be gained and encourages you to think that you're incapable of growing and ultimately reflects your "personality" of a fixed perspective. The voice affirms the belief system that are associated with a fixed mind and reiterates these in every occasion. The voice constantly searches to prove to prove that the beliefs you hold are correct and you must avoid growing. This voice is often an extremely toxic and restrictive voice that can cause more than a deficiency of motivation. It can cause a loss of self-esteem, an absence of self-confidence, an increase in chance of depression and anxiety as well as an increase in your levels of stress.

The voice you hear is likely to speak to you much more often than you think you are hearing, and it's important to be aware of what time and location it's speaking to you. One of the best ways to accomplish this step is to maintain a notebook or notepad in your smartphone which you can add to. When you are aware of your fix-minded voice talking to you, take a moment and record it. It is important to note down what your limiting idea is and also why you were influenced by this belief.

Note down everything you can think of even if the words sound negative or is incorrect. As an example, suppose you was to be said that "Of course, you failed," it's impossible to master things new. So why do you bother? Your failure is over And now, you're looking foolish and you look silly, too. The world should make you feel ashamed." The act of voicing this loudly to ourselves is extremely difficult, yet we frequently do not realize that speaking to ourselves is difficult. We've become accustomed to hearing this voice that we're numb. It's difficult to admit that we have this voice. However, it is the first step to cultivating a the mindset of growth. The first step is to acknowledge what is the "problem" and be willing to work to truly learn about ways you can change this aspect of you.

Recording the beliefs, the words that the voice was saying, as well as the trigger which caused the belief to start triggering will help you determine the reason you feel this voice is speaking to you. When you take the time to write these down, the faster you'll be able to identify changes in the triggers. Also the more mindful you develop of this voice, and the more easy you will be able to recognize the more complex and obscure triggers.

Be patient with this procedure. It is recommended that you allow it to last at the very least one month. But, in the event that you remember your growth mindset, it is something we continuously strive towards, and is not something that you can achieve. For the first time, one month should suffice for you to identify the voice you are hearing and eliminate it. You must keep a close eye on the voice you are hearing and work toward getting rid of it. The more you focus towards a more positive perspective, the more often you'll be able to recognize the voice that is limiting. The cycle is never over which is why you shouldn't be expecting that you will "finish" it during this procedure.

Instead, you should sit with it so that you can gain an understanding of your voice and its impact on the person you're listening to it so you're able to be a positive influence during the transition from a fixed mindset towards a growth mentality.

Make The Conscious Choice

The second step of the process is to select your growth-oriented mindset. If you've had a set mindset for a long time it's simple to lose sight of the fact that you are entitled to take a choice and that the decision you make has credibility and holds a place within your own life. Your decision is entirely yours to make. you interpret your experiences as well as the setbacks and difficulties. Up until now, you've decided to be critical of yourself, and see the obstacles as weaknesses and obstacles on your way. Yet, just like you've always been to make a choice, now you are able to look at these as learning opportunities instead.

If you are looking to achieve the success you desire in this change, you must make a conscious decision to develop a positive mentality. However, this doesn't mean you'll never be able to experience effects of a fixed-minded mindset in the future, but it does mean when you begin to notice the signs, you will need be making a conscious effort to eradicate these and develop a more positive perspective. They will be seen as learning opportunities and opportunities instead of limitations and obstacles. That is the case for every other thing which could hinder you from what you would like to accomplish. Instead of seeing everything which arises as a resounding obstacle, choose to view it as a learning experience and opportunity to learn. You must be able to accept the challenge as well as the chance to participate in the process of learning. That will guarantee that you're fostering the mindset of growing.

Listen to Your Growth Mindset "Voice"

As you do with a fixed-minded voice as well, you possess a growth-oriented voice. If you're hoping to experience the success of transforming from a fixed-minded to a the growth mindset, then you need practice listening to your growth-oriented mentality. It might be difficult because you've been neglecting this for too long, however trust it's within you.

The most effective way to develop your mental health is to speak it out loudly. As it's not been heard for a long time and it is silent enough that you can't be able to hear it. It is important to select the thought consciously and, more importantly the best way to do this is to use the technique as a way to "talk back" to your fixed-minded mindset. Each time you encounter thoughts of a fixed mental state then allow your growth idea to emerge and utilize the thought as a way to "correct" the fixed mindset thinking. You may feel as if that you're talking about yourself first however the more you utilize this technique, the simpler to change your mindset. It is the most effective method to recognize your old mentality and change it to your growth mindset.

Begin the Development Phase

When you've successfully recognized your fixed mentality and know where it's starting from, you are able to begin to develop. This is the process in which you're using specific methods and strategies that will "combat" your fixed mindset and begin replacing the fixed mindset with a more growth-oriented one completely. Additionally, it will assist you to improve and grow your mindset to become strong and encompassing.

Keep in mind that the entire journey will be one that you'll be able to repeat many times. The very first step of the process really is transformational because, possibly for the first time you're choosing a an attitude of growth. It is an enormous change for anyone, and it is important to recognize that within your own life. Know that, despite this, there are many occasions that you will notice changes in behavior patterns that are fixed and you have to change them by adopting growing mindset-based behaviors. Make sure you are working in this manner to identify the fixed-mind voice, addressing it using a grow-minded voice, and finally employing specific tools for development and techniques to change your fixed mindset by embracing healthier, more positive behavior patterns and habits of growth.

In this way, you won't just identify fixed-mind patterns but also get rid of the ones that aren't working and replace them with healthier ones as well. It is important to ensure that you're not just eliminating limitations or negative patterns, instead, you're changing them into healthier, growing patterning. This will avoid returning to fixed thinking pattern.

The transition from fixed to the growth mindset is a process that takes time and isn't "complete." You will continue to work on the process of transformation, so allow yourself the time and space. This is the perfect opportunity to develop a the growth mindset because you'll be required to invest in and be involved in the process. You will also need to learn to be able to forgive yourself when you make mistakes, and to honor your own self, no matter how stupid or ashamed you may be feeling. If you are able to honor yourself and accept these aspects during the process of transformation and growth process, the more you'll develop your mindset for growth. Consider it as element of the procedure. The more slow and compassionately you are moving, the quicker you'll progress.

Chapter 13: Developing Your Growth Mindset

The process of actually forming your mindset requires patience, time and regular the ability to practice. The process continues. It is essential to get up each morning and make an effort to develop an evolving mindset, and strive to develop it each and each day. As you take it on as a regular day-to-day event and accept the process as it is, the greater success you're will have in all of the steps. Take your time, be patient, and love yourself and be open to whatever happens during the process. It will help you are successful in your growing perspective. The strategies and methods listed below can help you make sure that you are able to build your mindset for growth by implementing specific, deliberate behaviour habits.

Embrace Imperfection

The trait of perfectionism is most common among people with a fixed outlook. This is the same characteristic that holds those who are fixed from learning any new thing. If you wish to cultivate a mindset of improvement then you must recognize the imperfections you have and accept your imperfections and embrace them. Accept that no individual is perfect in every way. Even those who excel at something aren't always flawless at their job since "perfect" does not truly exist. There's no such thing as being perfect at things.

Know that there's bound to make errors throughout the process and you'll encounter challenges as well as obstacles. Be prepared to see these challenges as a chance to learn from your mistakes, and accept your imperfect experience throughout the process. If you are able to accept the reality of life, the greater chance you'll be cultivating the growth attitude.

Reframe Your Perceptions

A lot of times, we are under the wrong impression that a mistake or missed opportunity must be considered an "failure" or a "final ending" of some thing. They are seen as an end in themselves and conclude that there's an impossible way for us to proceed or continue to our goal following a mishap or missed chance. It is one of the main symptoms of having a fixed mentality.

If you are looking to develop an attitude of growth it is essential to be able to reconsider your beliefs. It is possible to do this by asking yourself "What can I learn from this?" or "What is the lesson here?" When something happens to happen to not your liking. Rethinking your perspective to see obstacles and setbacks as an opportunity to learn and not as mistakes is the most effective method to make sure you are always able to see the learning possibilities in your life, and to ensure that you're not limiting yourself by self-limiting thoughts.

Learn New Things Often

No matter if you feel you need to master a new skill or not, you should practice the new skills regularly. Whatever size or tiny it may seem try to acquire a new skill every day. Develop your skills and dedicate yourself to each day. Be sure to be constantly acquiring new abilities and learning about new topics. That is how you will create neural pathways that are new to the brain. That is an important aspect of what a growing mindset means.

Avoid Seeking Approval

The reason many people are stuck in a certain attitude is that they're obsessed with getting the approval of their peers and of them. Their obsession leads to them fearing to appear stupid, foolish or incompetent in the eyes anyone since this would be a sign that they won't receive the approval of others. Additionally, they frequently believe that the reactions of others are indicative of approval when in actual it is not connected to either approval or disapproval and is instead a result of one specific event.

Individuals who seek approval from others usually do not take the necessary action due to they fear getting the approval of other people and in their own. If you are looking to develop a the growth mindset and make use of it in your personal daily life, it is essential to stop believing that you will achieve approval from anyone. The approval of others is not important as long as you have the right experiences and procedures.

Value the Process More

People who have a growing mindsets are extremely interested in the growth process. That is where learning process, the lessons as well as the experiences of life originate from. Learning creates memories as well as experiences and memories are created and new capabilities are developed. People who have an attitude of growth recognize this and will be more inclined to cherish learning over the rewards. While the reward can be beneficial, it's not the main goal of their effort. The process is worth it and putting your time and energy into this is the only way you're likely to discover opportunities to improve your enjoyment satisfaction, meaning, and enjoyment of your life.

People who have a fixed mentality have a tendency to avoid this aspect, yet it is actually the most significant and satisfying element of learning any subject. If you can let go of the necessity to be admired and put an emphasis and value to the learning process and the process, you'll likely see an increase in the happiness and fulfillment you feel through your day, which means that you'll enjoy a higher satisfaction with your life in general.

Own Your Purpose

The reason you are here is not likely to be similar to someone or anyone else's. This is the reason it's so crucial to never place importance on the acceptance of other people, or being able to count on the approval of others. When you know what your mission is and work toward the goal, you're more likely to feel a sense of satisfaction with yourself which means you'll have more purpose throughout your life. Thus, the more that you take ownership of your goals is the higher it will become. Being aware of your goals is one of the most important aspects in fostering a mindset of growth. This is often an important factor in expansion, so put the most importance and focus on this aspect of the procedure.

Emphasize on Your Growth

When you're just changing from a fixed-minded mindset to a growing mindset, you could notice yourself placing an importance on speed. "How fast can I do this?" could be a thought you have, but often. It is due to the fixed-mind people tend to be more concerned with their rewards rather than on the process. If you wish to adopt the mindset of a grower it is necessary to shift the focus of your attention from rewards toward the progress itself. Make sure you are focused on increase. Then, you should ask you "How much can I grow from this?" as well as "How can I maximize my growth from this experience?" If you can do that then you can successfully shift to the mindset of growth, and set the emphasis on growing. It will help you to develop which, as you've guessed that is the primary goal of having a mindset that is growth-oriented.

Reflect Regularly

The best way to reflect is to determine if you're getting the results you wish to achieve, or whether your growth isn't in the way you should be. Reflect on your life in order to determine what you've accomplished in your development and what your strengths and weaknesses lie. This is the perfect moment to look at any stuck thinking patterns in your mind and then work on healing them.

Abandon the "Ideal Image"

What is the "ideal image" of whom individuals are suppose to be, and how is expected of us to look is often the place where perfectionists and fixed-minds have their roots. If you're looking to let go of rigidity and cultivate a the growth mindset, you have be ready to give up the ideal self and be aware of who you wish to become in the future and your ultimate view of yourself is. Work towards improvement that gets you there.

Consistently Set New Goals

Goals can be significant factors for those who have a growth mindset. If you're able to accept your goals and set them for yourself on a regularly, it is almost certain that you'll gain knowledge. If in the opposite, then you're not setting goals high enough. Be prepared to make objectives and pursue these goals regularly. Each time you achieve the goal, make an additional goal. Keep a couple available every moment to ensure that you always have goals to focus on. If you aren't sure what number is sufficient concentrate on working towards only one short-term objective along with one medium-term goal, as well as one long-term target every day. It will ensure that you're always taking on new challenges regardless of size.

Be Realistic

The people who are growth-minded focused are realistic about their lives. They realize that one mistake an obstacle, setback or failure won't hinder them from seeing the big overall picture. They realize that no one is going to keep a record of one small error or a minor incident which could be embarrassing or unsettling to their personal lives. Instead, they accept that life is what it is. They put the things in perspective and keep their outlook. They don't allow anything to stand against the growth they desire or dreams as they realize that the size of the growth they are experiencing. Thus, nothing is large enough to stop their progress.

Growing mindset is a long-term process, and it's a continuous exercise. It is possible that at times you are able to cultivate a mindset of growth, at other times, it's tougher. In general, those tough moments is the time you have to be most active as that is when the best opportunities for growth are available. Be patient, remain focussed, and keep practicing regularly and you'll be successful in developing your personal mentality of growth.

Chapter 14: Difference Between Personality And Character

In the course of human evolution, we might become more advanced humans, but the basic instinct to feel at home with familiar objects to feel secure been lost to us. Perhaps that's one reason why we are compelled to categorize people into small classifications. This way, we feel you know them, and are in good hands for our surroundings. If we are asked to describe people, we generally describe them as imaginative, soft-spoken and gentle. It is possible to say that they are hostile, distant or cold.

Personality Mark is extremely enthusiastic. He is constantly encountering new people, never at home, and is always in motion He's a true go-getter. Every time I'm with Mark, I feel energized. I'm working with Mark.

Personality - Mark is not a listener to what I have to say, and we're never at a table by ourselves. He welcomes guests to sit with us, chats to those around us and doesn't pay any interest in me.

That's right, Mark started off as charming, enthusiastic person, however his partner realized that she could never have a relationship with him in the way she would like as he could have a tendency to overextend his relationships with other people.

People usually notice their characteristics before noticing some aspect of their character. These are only a symptom of the person's personality which may not have anything related to the person's nature. It is possible that we only have the opportunity to observe the person in a situation where they're at risk of being aggressive or they're experiencing difficult times that have resulted in them becoming distant and cold. The process of getting to know someone can be a challenge, as we think it is. People like to make judgments fast, in order that we feel secure, not realizing that we could judge someone without much details. This is how others judge us, except that we are able to help by providing proof of our character or lack thereof. Therefore, when you talk to someone should provide them with a more about yourself. It's not enough just to let the world know who you are and what interests you. It is important to demonstrate your morality.

Instead of saying that I'm the mother of two boys, four and six. The sad thing is that I get to see them at weekends, you could declare: I'm a father of two boys aged 6 and 4. I am grateful for every minute that I get to spend with them. I have so little of my time and I strive to make the most out of the time I have. This second one shows that you're an excellent father who enjoys spending time with his kids and the first let people know your sad account, and not divulge your innermost thoughts. When you are interviewing For instance, if you speak about your former work, you shouldn't mention things such as: it was demanding, it wasn't enjoyable or I was not driven. Instead, make use of sentences that describe similar issues, however this time you'll be able to describe your moral perspective that led the decision to leave your job. For example, you could say: I think that people behave indecently when they are in stressful situations. I would like to be in an office in which we work with each other to achieve a common goal and instead of pushing each other away at the beginning of a step. If I'm energized and feel motivated enough I transform into an engine that is well-oiled. It's not necessary to be concerned about my ability to get the task completed, so you have an end goal in your mind.

Chapter 15: 12 Pillars Of Character

Like architects must build a solid foundation in order for constructing a large structure Your character also requires foundations upon which to develop a robust character. These 12 pillars will make your confidence, pride and tall throughout the course of your days with the knowledge that what you leave in your wake is done by courtesy and a sense of virtuosity from your side. They are complicated attitudes and behaviors, and we'll attempt to clarify how to better balance the two, and not push the extremes.

I-III: Courage, Adult Bullying, Respect

Gutsy Hero or a Full-Blown Fool? What are your strengths?

Courage is a relative concept. It is a time when bravery when it is pushed to the limit is admired, even if it's not praised. If you attempt to get away from your friend's father from the second-story window of their home and you are hailed as hero-like until you graduate high school. As a mature, well-adjusted person If you're not someone who is a drug dealer or firefighter, throwing yourself out of windows is not something you ought to perform to prove any kind or point. In adulthood, you must display the courage to stand up for yourself. Make sure everyone knows that there's a right path, and you're on the right path. Let people know your thoughts. However, this doesn't mean that you have to be a shrewd, honest person and ramming your thoughts down others throats. It's not the way of old Greece where individuals were permitted to sit for hours on the area of parliament to voice their opinions. Nowadays it is likely that you will encounter a fool who is bigger than you. If the workplace Gossip Girls meet to share their thoughts on upon someone You can freely express the world your opinion about office gossip as well as their lack of effectiveness.

Get the courage to follow your desires. Do not give up and allow others to perform your work, since this shows that you're not in control of your existence. There is no the control of your life If you let other people take advantage of you, there is a chance to be a winner. It doesn't mean you have to compete with everybody to be the most successful at anything. You should only fight for things you cherish. If you've got a strategy and are confident in the course of your endeavors, incredible courage is going to propel ahead and inspire you to keep moving forward. This will show the people who is around that you're fully engaged and striving to achieve your goals. Make your own choices. Sometimes, your bold and enthusiastic attitude can draw you to your workplace and lock you up at your workstation. It happens most often because you're trying you to please your employer (or any other person) by your tenacity and commitment to the job. You accept more responsibility than you're capable of. The result is lots of work. A lot of work could result in a lot of errors over the duration of the. Look for the top priorities within your own life then complete them step one at a time.

Your Tongue Is Not Made Of Steel, but It Cuts

Our minds are filled with pimples, hormone-filled teenagers when we talk about"bully," but adults are much more vicious bullies than children. Most adults do not even know they're being bullied or they're being abused. Employers are often bullied by bosses and many do not realize that their workplace is far less stress-free than it ought to be. If you're employed at an institution, shouting or directing people to move around could be lifesaving for someone. If you manage the office of administration in your business, and the task you're supposed to get executed today is completed within a week and nobody will notice, do not yell at your employees to let everyone know who's the superior. If you are viewed as a threat to those that are afraid of your actions, you'll appear to become a small-minded ignorant simpleton who loves creating discomfort. As an adult, battling bullies is a lot easier than it was when you were a child. It is not necessary to worry about whether they will assault you physically in the event that you're in danger or dangerous situation.

Adult bullying has more sophistication than bullying in schools. In the past the wedgies or swirlies were popular. For adults it is hard to believe that someone would have did these things to you prior to when they took it to the next level. There are a variety of adult kinds of bullying. And the majority of bullies employ a handful examples to impress you. The deliberate sabotage of others, denial of merit, capability or value or ignoring a person and disregarding their friendship, the good will of others are all methods utilized by adult bullies. These are all signs that you have no clue about what's going on behind your eyes, and that you aren't concerned about the other person's opinions and their lives. It's possible to think of people who are close to you and you might even be a bit smitten every time one of your new acquaintances call to ask to meet however, in their eyes they will see you as showing incredible disdain for the fact they took a portion of their day time with you and didn't be more uncaring. You could be wasting the entire time of your friends telling your personal story, without ever asking them how their divorce progressing. Everyone does this, and that doesn't necessarily mean you're a bad person. But if you're doing this often, or employ various bullying tactics it is time to think about what got you off the path of excellence. Then, what is the most efficient way to return.

Respect Everybody, And Yourself

Einstein declared that we should speak with everyone the same manner, regardless of no matter if they're the head of the university or the trash man. There are many books published on this topic as it is one of the only ways people can show that they're an individual within the universe that we are. Avoid talking about people negatively or ignoring anyone because you believe you're worth more than them in any way. The issue isn't about the person who was offended but about yourself. If you do not want being around people who are poor, uninformed or unemployed, you're not offending them in the same way that you're offending yourself. You believe that without money or degree, or achievement or accomplishments, you're unworthy of the respect you deserve. In the same way that you've got triumphs and failures others are also able to share their experiences. It is important to respect one another due to the fact that it is easy to find yourself with them and the reverse is also true. Our world today is an uncertain one and the luck you have may change at any moment. Never forget your origins and the path you took to get there.

It is important to show respect regardless of the situation as well as to anyone who you encounter in your day-to-day everyday life. Respect lets people know that you allow them be as they are and your progress has nothing to do with have to do with their own development. Be considerate of anyone, old or young rich, poor, those with and lacking the same character. In order to be able to accomplish this and be respectful of everyone you meet, you first must respect yourself. It's a simple thing to believe, but if you take a moment to think about it, you'll realize that there were times in your life that you didn't feel particularly proud of yourself and you shouldn't be giving you any credit. The concept of respect was created to hide the areas which don't allow for affection. Therefore, if there are aspects that you do not completely appreciate, it's possible to come up with reasons to admire the person you don't love. This is the same thing for those who refuse to give anyone room to honor those aspects of themselves. If you have to do so, look for something that resonates with your current state of mind. If they're doing something that's detrimental in your relationship, let them know that you'd like them to change their behavior and prove that you are still in love. Except if you aren't interested and in that case getting away from them is the ideal choice for you both. You could be in the category of blaming yourself as in the case of situations where you don't pay attention to yourself or your requires to be able to satisfy the needs of someone else.

IV-VI: Tolerance, Fairness, Honesty

The tales of tolerance go back prior to the Christian church. However, it appears that we're facing different forms of prejudice each century. In this time of history is when we've changed to hatred towards Muslims. 100 years ago that was when it was the African Americans, before that it was the Indians and the Jews and the witches prior to them we targeted those who were not Christians as well as the

Christians as well as the other Christians. The list of names could stretch all the way back to Adam or Eve. Each generation is a brand new list of hates and this is something you can tackle with patience and compassion.

We are evolving into an egomaniac population. People who want to have it all and to be the first in order to have more. The world is not treated world with fairness because we're unfair to ourselves. It is impossible to be the best at everything always. It's unreasonable to aim at everything in pursuit of success. Is it right and rational to allow athletes, priests as well as politicians to put millions of dollars into their accounts in the midst of nearly half the globe is struggling to survive? Do not be selfish and greedy. The people who have an excess of money that they cannot spend are engaged in an ongoing battle within their minds. They know in their heart that all they require is an adequate roof and food to eat. The rest is just extra like the anxiety over loosing the accumulation and also the subliminal moral hazard of possessing an item that is taken by someone who requires the item. It's not necessary to feel that threatening tension in your mind while you are able to cruise your boat with calm sky.

It is common for us to believe that we require more. In today's society, the quantity of goods outweighs the quality. Instead of being focused solely on one job our minds are constantly occupied with multiple tasks. We are able to make friends in a bar, and not the one with whom who has been with us throughout the thick and thin. Social media replaced genuine friendships and love was replaced by superficial sexual relations. The truth is that you lie to yourself in order in order to conceal an neglected wound. If you lie to yourself and your mind tries to interpret the lie as true until it's no longer able to distinguish between what's true and what's not. If the truth is handed to you there will be doubts on its validity, as the mind is conditioned to recognizing truth as inauthentic. If you're honest with yourself, then you are open to people around you with a sincere and kind approach.

VII-IX: Caring, Compassion, Kindness

Imagine how your mornings will go if your companion serves you coffee every day and your bellboy is there to open the door to you to wish you a prosperous day. The receptionist greets you with a genuine smile and the day keeps running smoothly throughout the day without you seeing the rage of your face. It happens to everyone particularly in film industry. In real life it is commonplace to rush to somewhere else, and rarely engaging in any meaningful interactions with people we meet before continuing to go to another place. Every once in a rare blue moon, we take a moment to think about the things that matter which keep us satisfied. What makes us smile, it's common to discover a moment in time where we've made another person satisfied. It's the best joy you could ever experience. that feeling of making people happy due to the actions you took. It is possible to buy high-end footwear all you like however if you purchase shoes for someone else who truly would like them, the happiness is multiplied. Our actions leave an impression on others around us through what we do in addition to the words we talk about. However, words can make a difference to an individual's life or day instantly. It is impossible to know the extent of your words of encouragement can change the perspective of someone else, or perhaps these were the exact words that they required hearing the most during that time.

There are many people who have lost the ability to feel empathy. As a result, they are unable to show compassion. Their smiles don't reflect their true feelings or their speech isn't sincere. They aren't able to communicate the proper emotional response to a particular scenario, and the interaction never feels natural. There is a Dalai Lama said that this perpetual period of conflict and violence could be eliminated in perpetuity if a generation of kids learns to practice meditation. According to him, through the practice of meditation, one can begin to feel as if you are an integral part of the globe, and the whole world. If you can realize that the fact that you're member of something that everyone has become an integral part of, then there is no way to harm anyone else. Since you'll hurt you too. Being kind, compassionate and thoughtful is rewarded in the exact similar way. This is not just because people are friendly to you as well however, you are always attracted by the people on the same wavelength like you, but rather because these are positive feelings which push negative feelings away.

Make sure you are kind to all people that you come across. It is a way to be kind on multiple different levels. It can connect the spiritual side of your souls and help you rise into a state that you are aware of their positive quality in their smiles and their facial expressions. It is a way to put playing poker with who have negative thoughts. Because they view reality through dim, dark glasses Your kindness may appear to be a ploy you're trying to play. Be kind to them and don't be harsh with their actions. They may not have had the opportunities to meet people at your speed and so, share your Apple joy to your friends. Let them see your serene nature by sharing a smile, real human connection, and sincere phrases. Perhaps you'll give a lost soul that a brighter path than the one they're accustomed to: an outline of the highest road.

X-XII: Trustworthiness, Responsibility, Perseverance

There's nothing better than having confidence in somebody. You can be confident that whatever's going on with you, either good or bad it will always be in an enclave of safety in their home, heart and hands. Wouldn't you like to have a sidekick and a helping hand an amiable confidant? If you'd like to have someone like this to be in your life, then it is your responsibility to become the person's confidant, helper and even a side kick. If you're in a relationship that is reciprocal will be able to completely release the doubts and fears that you have and be able to trust them or even be able to trust them. Do something to show the world that you are trustworthy. It is possible to use your words to draw attention of others, but your actions are an eternal mark upon your personality.

When you get the opportunity to demonstrate that you're a gentleman or woman of moral character, don't take your obligation to be lightly. When your peers trust you to carry out an act, making a mistake that is not justified can make you look like a weak connection. Make sure you are in charge of any tasks you're working on regardless of whether it's a brand partnership, promotions or even a plan for training. So, in the event that things go wrong at some point in the future it will be possible to say that you tried your best and remain committed until the final. A person who is right for you are able to tell the fact that you've held your own and will respect your decision for the right reasons.

This won't go as smoothly everywhere you go there are difficulties. It's important to demonstrate persistence, not only due to the fact that you need to come back from every loss and succeed, but also because it increases the stamina of your muscles. The effort you put into it will be rewarded since with each loss you acquire experience. The reason why people say that life's like an online game. The quests can be repeated when playing a video game provided you be able to pass the test in order to locate the reward. In the real world it is possible that you won't be able to return to the time of your choice and re-do the actions you've taken, however there are a myriad of actions that are possible in real life. Virtual reality is finite, whereas in real life, possibilities are limitless. There is always an alternative route, create an entirely new plan or employ a distinctive pickup strategy. If your attention on the things that you aren't able to do, instead of what you are able to do and do, your mind will attempt to aid your thinking process by giving you examples of things you aren't able to perform, or are scared of, or aren't prepared to do. If you let that thought train running through your head the chances are you'll be wasting time, energy and lose the chance to take advantage of amazing opportunities.

Chapter 16: Be A Good Citizen - Good Citizen Vs Bad Citizen

What defines a great citizen has been questioned several times by human beings, like us, as well as famous figures that had a major impact on the evolution of humans. The definition of a citizen is someone who can do his best, since every person that is doing their best contributes to a stronger country. Accepting this as a rule of thumb that you must do the best you can to not be the burden for society. No matter what, never regardless of whether you're disabled or have been deemed older. There are lots of ways to contribute to the society while contributing to your life. It is possible to volunteer, deliver talks, or offer assistance in shelters, and transform the world, one step by step.

Someone thought up the idea of opening an unread library. People who go to this library share their stories, instead of having them written down through books. Make a library just like the one shown here. It's an inspiring idea and also a sanctuary for many. Older people, veterans wandering souls, lonely A lot of people will feel a sense of relief as the most we really need is for our stories to be known. Find ways to assist your community grow and be more harmonious. Make sure you are a responsible neighbour and take care of the environmental surroundings. Be mindful of how much you're able to eat, and do not waste resources, and don't leave litter wherever you travel. Find ways to be a force for good in the same way as President Roosevelt stated. Look for ways to assist the entire community pull its weight as well. Create a program which will take food waste at restaurants, and then donate the food to shelters for animals. Start a daycare centre and help elderly houses, and connect both the weak and connections that are strong. Our goal is to help each other learn and support each other in how to live our lives. If a person isn't prepared for your dose of ethical behavior and conduct, do the best you can to stay clear of the person. The saying goes that unhygienic relationships ruin good character It's true.

Be informed of the world that you reside within. The Holocaust was a fact that came to the eye of all the globe, yet people were ignorant and allowed one tiny man to roaming Europe in the form of a wicked pope in the middle ages. All of us are in the same boat. you must be on the lookout for signs that the ship gets sunk. Learn about your rights as a person of the nation and cast your make a vote. Be informed of the political climate within your country and discover ways to stay clear of these cleverly designed traps.

Nowadays, nearly every government in the world is corrupt, and presides over its citizens in some manner So, find methods to avoid the tricks they employ. Keep in mind the law and respect the space and property of the other citizens as well as be accountable to your conduct. Be accountable for what you're accountable for, irrespective of whether that's your actions or words. Be aware of your rights and do not permit anyone else to profit from your property or you. If you believe that the government is in error in a way that is detrimental to us all as a whole Your vote is important only if you are part of those who. They are the people on the streets, those whom you are asked to sign petitions take part in their activities and build a better world in which everyone is equally.

A good citizen is things that are different across different regions around the world.

Some places wherein Japan that you won't be allowed to dance even if you choose to you will be deemed as a violation of the law and you could find your expulsion. If you plan to set up an establishment there, in which customers are allowed to dance, then you'll require an additional license. Protesting openly against discrimination based on sexuality is regarded as good citizenship in a lot of countries, however in a few, you can get stoned to death. The law requires you to adhere to the rules and traditions of other nations, so provided they're fair and do not affect the growth of the nation. If you are able to do something that will change the globe, it's your obligation to take action. Then you will become a responsible citizen, a globalist and an exemplary citizen of our world.

One of the chapters in the Bhagavad Gita focuses on the lower self and the Higher

Self within every one of us. The lower self is comprised of the body's physical form, brain and the senses. Your body is what you nourish and nurture is able to be a vehicle to go places, look around, and also encounter experiences that help reconnect your mind to your soul. The soul, or your inner self, is the Self that God has that is mentioned in the Gita. If this Self isn't in charge over the mind, body and the senses, you will never be able to feel God. It is necessary allow your Higher Self to expand and show its fullness. It's your link to God as the Divine or greater energy. If you allow your lower Self guide you on this journey called life, you'll experience just the pleasures of earth and primitive emotions such as the desire to be a victim of envy, greed as well as ignorance, jealousy, and self-confidence. Your self-image will become falsely centered in a false sense and render your life on earth useless.

It's exactly what the Gitas affirm it, and one doesn't need to adhere to the Hindu faith for the fundamental idea to be understood. In particular, since it pertains to the traits we consider to be the ideal qualities of a human being. You should never overindulge the senses to often. It is important to choose self-control instead of the anger and envy and to truly be present within your world, and without any false pretense of self-importance and pride. Also, create a true relationship with those who surround you. In order to break free of the bonds that we have with the material world, and allow ourselves to be in a state of higher consciousness of Being. The state of being enlightened, in which your mind and senses are guided by your highest self, which is the real You.

Chapter 17: Be Yourself

The expression Be Yourself has so much acceptance within the idea. It's short and simple, but is so misunderstood by a lot of us. It says you must be who you are. It can be used as a reason against many amoral people in order to justify their sinister actions. A lot of people find comfort within these phrases, even if they've committed more sins than they could ever be sorry for. If you're seeking to improve as a individual, it's okay to justify the old way of thinking. This means that you accept the fact that you've done something wrong throughout the years and attempt to find the balance. However, there are many individuals who are determined to continue performing the wrong actions since it's who they are. They'll believe they're doing their best to be themselves. They may blame their environment and genes, the society they live in as well as their own experiences and even yourself at times. Most likely, it's because of the fear that they won't confront the truth in those moment. They worry that they'll never be admired and respected as previously, and that they will get labelled and judged and be sacked of all legitimacy and credibility. If you're going to go this much as to be someone like them confront the true you before accepting it for what you are.

Are you the person you wish to be? Are you following the right path? Do you have plans to be to where you want to be? Are you taking steps to become the person you would like to become? Are you following your heart? You intuition? What was the last time you were able to reflect all of you here on earth? What do you do to makes you feel like a special snowflake? Do you do these things? Do you know what they do and the reason you aren't investigating all options? Have you let go of the fears you had? Are you ready to face them?

They can't be confronted If you continue to run away from them. This is the very first rule of the game. Both of you and your worries will bump into one another throughout your life. The key is to get the frightened ones before they do any injury. They could halt your growth in a variety of ways as they are just creatures. They'll hide your talent and abilities from you, or make you feel uncomfortable once you're confident, and then attempt to undo the whole of your existence. Remember that they're not given to you by an wicked God or the gods of the underworld. they're your creation. Your mind's creation. Certain thoughts can be dismissed while others will be laughed at while others might require all your attention. As time passes, you're bound to be confronted by them and you must prepare yourself with self-love and love. Uncover your inner child this spark that requires only just a breath to explode into flames.

It is likely that if you have discovered something that is intriguing, you'll be able to discover another within the next period of time. Therefore, you should try a variety of things. If you think that you are artistic, you must have an undiscovered talent in that. If you've attempted painting and you're adept at, is drawing, then remember that Banksy has become famous. It is important to find ways to expand your perspective. Find ways to stimulate your brain. For you to find a cause. There are a variety of activities and interests that you could discover intriguing. You can try writing, cooking video editing, or gardening. If you can't then you'll be able to have a beautiful gardening space to admire.

The issue we face as a group of individuals through the years was that we stopped being able to grow as individuals, with the advent of technology. Before, cooking, gardening as well as sewing and other arts and crafts were taught in schools. In Japan the students attend classes in hygiene, in which they wash their rooms and the facilities of their school. In the present, just a few of countries can prove that they have character development in their curriculum for schools. This is why today there are a myriad of arts and crafts that are threatened in a sense. The Guardian published a research in the past few years in which it was revealed that there was only one denim maker across the UK. Also, there's just one barrel maker for wood along with a clog maker. There are just two makers of scissors. It's not an argument to make the wool yourself and weaving yourself However, there are lots of areas where that you could dip your finger to see if the results make you feel happy.

It's among the most important indications that you're skilled in something. You're enjoying it! If you are a person who is enthusiastic about doing something then the odds of you getting it done well are a lot. Your intuition is the sound of your heart. It whispers softly of the things that we were made to accomplish, yet we seldom listen. It's unwise to take a break from your work making recycled paper even if your cards set. If it's something that you like doing, then follow your instincts and create the plan to get a pleasing outcome. Take note of that soft voice the next time. If it suggests you go a different way for the bank in the future try it. If your gaze is fixed to someone and your soul wants to greet them to them, smile. It's crucial to improve your intuition, as well as consider it as another or your senses. It will help you find your joy and what that you're good in. It will allow you to recognize the places which feel family and people that whom you trust totally.

If your gut instinct finally brings you back to the things that are right to be yours, the activities that you are passionate about spending your time with, you'll be relaxed and at peace with the surrounding world. This is who you really are and not the you everyone says is just who you really are! Once you're able to discern yourself, is it possible to be you. You should also be yourself all the time and in every scenario. Tell them the world who Terrence is and his goal. Make them aware that although you might appear tiny in comparison to the world, your own world is vast and constantly growing.

Chapter 18: Can Character Be Taught?

The current world is extremely difficult to comprehend and be in agreement on a universal idea of the good and the bad. Everyone is familiar with the 10 Commandments as well as the twelve pillars of character. There is no need to be a member of any religious group and they will have a place and are respected as general standards of conduct. These are the values we learn easily as children, and must continue to adhere to throughout our lives. But, not every one of us were fortunate enough to live in an environment that was safe and secure. We were all victims of abuse and crimes Many were treated poorly and washed up in the wilderness, and a lot of us went through times of hardship. This doesn't mean there isn't a sense of what is right and wrong, however, those who've sunk their feet to the bottom of the ocean typically have a clear view of the truth.

It's not often the case it is common for people to allow their experiences to change them, without ever touching the steering wheel. There are a lot of terrible incidents that happen to people each daily. Many of them could be happening to you. What's important is to not allow those experiences to ruin our character. The images you see to you may appear terrifying and more real than what we've seen in film industry. The images you see in your mind can occasionally alter the perspective of your eyes or your mindset and persona. Most of us go about our lives and do not think about the way our surroundings affect us and how it affects our lives and influences our timeline. Everybody is programmed either way. We are shaped by our experiences our interactions with people as well as the books we read and the people we admire. Our lives are shaped by our parents, our society that we reside in, and also the world we're born into.

Let's consider Hitler as an illustration. He believed that his actions were helping mankind by taking out anyone who did not meet his definition of a superior race. He believed that good is anybody, with or without characteristics, who was white in skin, beautiful eyes, and hair. The Catholic church believes that those who believe in atheism are the ones that aren't goodness, and according to the perspective of those who are atheists, God could not be be spotted within a church. The atheists may be able to see the kindness of others or in their smile at the dawn sun or in the wonder of their birth. There are many different views of what is good and bad, and nobody has ever done any act in the name of bad. Everyone is doing good depending on what we believe to be right.

But, all general guidelines are to be followed The world has been in conflict for the last many years due to our inability to reach a consensus on a universal idea of what is good. If you've experienced failed romantic relationships because you believed that you and your partners were lazy, and you needed to care for each of you your brain, things like laziness as well as procrastination and lack of discipline can be thought to be signs of someone who is not a personality. When you encounter somebody who's well-off and productive Your mind could play an illusion on you to convince you that they're people who have moral character when in reality they do not.

There's no way to erase every negative event, even if were tempted to. It's not a good idea. The brain needs more data, as it receives information from it. The software is installed inside our brains, from the time we were children, teens as well as when we first entered the workforce. There is no way to force your brain to get rid of this program However, you will be able to manage your reactions to them whenever they pop out. Your response to the experience is a reflection of your character. It is important to take a step back and examine your situation to see what it truly is. There is no limit to what you can do to accomplish, and developing a personality will be easy because it is something you do every day.

It is possible to meet individuals with an inaccurate view of goodness, and you can examine your progress. Don't compare what you have achieved to theirs. That would not be moral. However, you should be able to observe what your brain develops to make an idea that is good when you are within the context of a negative example. Always be honest with yourself and analyze your own experiences. Be honest with yourself, and observe the areas where you've displayed your character and good qualities, as well as the places where your unconscious mental processes create an issue. It is common for us to react in a subconscious way through our lives because we can identify the signals to be either positive or negative as well as believing that the same thing will occur its self.

There are always choices to decide what we do in response to other people or events. If someone shouts at you and you've programmed your mind to believe that fighting using identical weapons will win the war, then you'll be angry or engage in fighting. If you think it is not possible to win with shouts and kicking people around then you'll be able to soothe the individual in order to come up with a sensible answer. Making a person a better person is an ongoing process of learning. You will create and restore for you've lived your entire life.

www.ingramcontent.com/pod-product-compliance
Lightning Source LLC
Chambersburg PA
CBHW071442080526
44587CB00014B/1949